# THE SWEET LIFE

# *The Sweet Life*

## Natural Macrobiotic Desserts

Marcea Weber

Japan Publications, Inc.

*In Memory of Rose*
*my mother, teacher, friend*

© 1981 by Marcea Weber

Published by JAPAN PUBLICATIONS, INC., TOKYO

*Distributors:*

UNITED STATES: *Kodansha International/USA, Ltd., through Harper & Row, Publishers, Inc., 10 East 53rd Street, New York, New York 10022.* SOUTH AMERICA: *Harper & Row, Publishers, Inc., International Department.* CANADA: *Fitzhenry & Whiteside Ltd., 150 Lesmill Road, Don Mills, Ontario M3B 2T6.* MEXICO AND CENTRAL AMERICA: *HARLA S. A. de C. V., Apartado 30–546, Mexico 4, D. F.* BRITISH ISLES: *International Book Distributors Ltd., 66 Wood Lane End, Hemel Hempstead, Herts HP2 4RG.* EUROPEAN CONTINENT: *Boxerbooks, Inc., Limmatstrasse 111, 8031 Zurich.* AUSTRALIA AND NEW ZEALAND: *Book Wise (Australia) Pty. Ltd., 101 Argus Street, Cheltenham Victoria 3192.* THE FAR EAST AND JAPAN: *Japan Publications Trading Co., Ltd., 1–2–1, Sarugaku-cho, Chiyoda-ku, Tokyo 101.*

First edition: September 1981
Second printing: August 1983

*LCCC No. 80–84414*
*ISBN 0–87040–493–8*

Printed in U.S.A.

# FOREWORD

Marcea Weber came to Boston over ten years ago. From the beginning, she was a very active student of macrobiotic cooking, especially good quality desserts and sweets.

In Japan, we are not accustomed to eating sweets after our meals, so I did not have much experience with cooking desserts. As Marcea was studying how to substitute healthier ingredients and creating many beautiful and wonderful desserts, she inspired many others to try her delicious recipes and experiment themselves.

Marcea went to London with her husband and helped establish macrobiotic enterprises there. The Webers have a wonderful energy, which they later used to begin teaching in Sydney, Australia. While I have not yet visited their center, macrobiotic activity is strong and growing due to their efforts, which we appreciate very much. Marcea's presentation of the healthy way of cooking has benefited many people.

The Webers come back to Boston from time to time, lecturing in various places and encouraging many people. They have become very strong and healthy and we are grateful that they are sharing their experience, both by teaching and writing books.

AVELINE TOMOKO KUSHI

# INTRODUCTION

From Pure Joy Springs
all creation; by Joy
it is sustained, toward
Joy it proceeds and to
Joy it returns.

TANTRA ASANA

From Grandma's apple pie to chocolate hot fudge sundaes, desserts are an integral part of the American diet. However, what was once an occasional treat, has now become a national pastime.

In 1850, families consumed about two pounds of sugar a week. In 1900, most American families consumed five pounds of commercially "refined" sugar a week. This did not include the sugar in natural sources such as fruits, other vegetables and grains. Today, the average American family consumes more than four hundred pounds of sugar yearly—a very far cry from dear old Grandma's time.

I remember my mother, who was European and definitely a woman of the old school, filling the air with the aroma of her homemade breads, cakes, pastries, cookies and pies. She would usually bake on Fridays, baking enough bread for the coming week and an extra cake or pie or two as a special treat for us or the neighbors.

Using her own basic recipes and then elaborating on them, she would create pineapple-cherry upside-down cakes, honey-walnut cakes, fruit cakes, marble cakes, apple pies—there was no end to her ingenuity. In addition, she would always make something from dough that she could shape with her hands: turnovers, babkas, strudels, cookies—never measuring anything by the cup, but instead using her eyes and her intuition.

I never realized how much influence baking with my mother had on me until I began to bake by myself. I remember watching, fascinated, as her hands kneaded and shaped the strudels and turnovers, filling them with poppy seeds and prune butter, or with apples, raisins and nuts. Sometimes I helped, cleaning mixing bowls and spoons by licking them, cutting out cookies with an old glass, or just playing with the dough.

Today, in my kitchen I have returned to using the natural ingredients that my mother used when she first started making desserts as a young girl in Europe. She once told me the story of how she rarely had to go to the store in town to buy ingredients for baking. My father, her boyfriend at the time, grew wheat and millet on his farm a few houses away. She would get the grain from him and then bring it to her father, who would grind it into flour in his mill. Eggs she obtained from her chickens, milk from the family cow or goat, water from the well, and butter was freshly churned by her mother. Even sea salt was always in abundant supply because her cousin who lived near the ocean dried and sold it for a living. She never used refined sugar in her baking or dessert making but relied instead on honey or fresh fruits for sweetness and taste. When fruit was in season she would pick it and use it; when it wasn't in season it wasn't used.

When she came to America, everything changed. There were no flour mills close by where she could get freshly ground flour, no trees or vines to pick fresh fruit from, and she couldn't keep chickens, goats and cows in an apartment. No longer surrounded by foods in their natural state, she began to adapt to her new way of life, still trying to select the best quality products at the local stores. She had to choose from more refined packaged foods and settle for whatever fresh foods could be obtained.

When I began to bake it was even more difficult to find ingredients that were not only "natural," but wholesome as well. I discovered that every item I bought for cooking, baking or dessert making had something added as well as something taken away. Strange as it may seem, I never questioned "refined" foods until I became ill and a doctor recommended that I change my diet to regain my health. He strongly suggested that I substitute "natural" foods for refined foods and completely eliminate sugar from my diet, except for the sugar from natural sources such as fruits, grains and vegetables.

This suggestion lead me to a natural food store, where I began to read more labels. All was supposedly "natural" and, in most cases, "organic." There was no evidence of bleached or bromated flour. The oils were "crude" and "unrefined," they looked darker and smelled like what they were extracted from—the germ of corn, sesame, safflower, soybean or olive. Salt with its natural minerals was not refined with additives to make it "whiter" and "free-flowing." Spices were not adulterated with artificial coloring or preservatives, and were grown "organically" if possible.

Sugar was nowhere to be found. Sugar as we know it today is not in its natural state but is highly refined. Even the so-called "natural" or "raw" sugar has been refined and then colored back to brown, its original color, to make it look "natural." The only sweeteners found in the store were natural sugars such as maple syrup, fruit concentrates, honey, apple butter, apple juice or cider, barley malt extract and sorghum molasses.

Many of these products were labeled "natural," "unrefined" or "organic." Confused by these terms, I asked what they meant. The owner explained to me that "organic" means that the foods are grown without chemical fertilizers, synthetics, herbicides, fungicides, pesticides or any chemical at all. The farmer depends on the health and vitality of the plant to resist disease, and he uses natural fertilizers and cultivation methods to control the weeds. He further stated that these products were kept under natural conditions without the use of pesticides while they were being shipped to the store.

The word "natural" he explained, has an entirely different meaning. It means that no additives or preservatives of any kind have been added to the food after it is grown. He went on to say that many people today knowingly or unknowingly use chemical preservatives or additives without considering the effect these may have on their bodies. Many people have been convinced that additives will impart a better taste, color, texture and even aroma to foods. Often additives are used as a selling device to make foods more appealing to the senses. They are needed to enrich foods because the refining processes has stripped them of their natural vitamins and minerals. They are also added to prolong shelf life. He warned me that chemical additives may injure the body if ingested daily. Preservatives and additives, which are found in most refined products today, were not used years ago because food was preserved by natural methods such as canning, pickling or drying, or by using salt, a natural preservative. A small sign hanging on the wall in the store made it all clear: *Additives or preservatives should be harmless to man or they defeat their purpose.*

This book was written with these very words in mind. Ever since I discovered that food was directly responsible for the way that I thought, felt and developed, I have tried to obtain the freshest and purest ingredients possible.

Since desserts are an integral part of most of our diets today, it is necessary that they should be as wholesome and nutritious as possible. Yet they should still remain an occassional treat—something to look forward to at the end of a meal! *But not every meal!*

Our bodies know what we need, and if we are in tune with nature, then we will understand what we must have. We do not receive nourishment only through the food that we put in our mouths, but also through exercise, sunshine, clean air, rest, as well as tears and laughter. *This is all food.*

So, in the silence of your kitchen, you should accept with gratitude the honor of being able to cook for one, two or even ten. What you give of yourself when cooking is what your friends and family will receive in eating. It is very important that you care about what you are doing and create with utmost joy, laughter and love— and let the sun shine in.

# ACKNOWLEDGMENT

As this book goes into it's second printing, it is almost impossible to list each and every person responsible for helping to create the rebirth of this manuscript.

My deep appreciation goes primarily to all of my teachers who helped to change my direction: George and Lima Ohsawa, Michio and Aveline Kushi, Herman and Cornellia Aihara, and my mother and father: Rose and Paul, who made it all possible.

The other side of the scale is balanced by my dear friends who allowed me to use their sense of taste, smell, sight, touch and hearing to create the recipes.

When it seemed as if the end of editing, typing, and re-typing would never be in sight, Barbara and Susan helped lighten the load by sharing the tasks.

Thanks also to Kathleen, who stopped whatever she was doing to "quickly" read the latest blurb of inspiration from the typewriter, and to Daniel, my dear husband, who has the patience to wait, the strength to make me continue, and the constitution to taste (and survive) the recipes.

A very special word and heartfelt gratitude to Leonie Moat, who along with her exquisite illustrations, and sense of design and color, also gave me her experience, intuition, and understanding. Truly, this book would not have been possible without her support and friendship.

And last, but not least, you, who created a need that I could supply, with great joy.

Thank you.

# CONTENTS

# 1. NATURAL NECESSITIES: Equipment, Techniques and Ingredients

## Necessary Equipment

*Aluminum utensils can be dangerous to your health*

Just as good natural foods make more nutritious desserts, proper kitchen tools are necessary for the preparation of good quality culinary delights. By using the cooking and baking utensils suggested, you will find that your desserts are not only more delectable, but truly wholesome as well.

J.P. Beach, editor of the magazine *You and Your Health*, has pointed out that aluminum "exerts an irritating action on the mucosa of the entire gastrointestinal tract before absorption, and, as aluminum salts, on the tissues and organs of the body after absorption. Thus, it is a common cause of constipation, colitis, and ulcers . . . "

Aluminum and aluminum compounds formed in cooking, he says, combine with alkaline saliva and the alkaline juices of the duodenum to create gas. (Similarly, many commercial bakers use aluminum to blow up products and make them light.) This gas-making process is continued throughout the digestive system, irritating and damaging tissue. "These poisons," Beach says, "back up into the liver and kidneys and produce the symptoms of metallic poisoning."

Aluminum and the aluminum compounds, Beach goes on, also destroy vitamins in food (testified by Docket No. 540, Federal Trade Commission, Washington D.C.).

If you boil ordinary drinking water in an aluminum dish or pan for half an hour and immediately pour it into a clear glass container, you can see the aluminum compounds, mostly aluminum hydroxide. In cooking, more of these particles are released from the aluminum, enter into the food, and are absorbed by the body as well.

I recommend that you choose baking and cooking utensils made of earthenware, stoneware, porcelain, cast iron, enamel or glass. Avoid aluminum and all synthetically coated equipment. For the same reason, avoid wrapping food in aluminum foil for baking, cooking or storing.

*Mixing*

Glass or porcelain mixing bowls
Wooden spoons
Measuring cups, stainless steel or tin for dry ingredients, and glass for liquids
Measuring spoons
Flour sifter or strainer
Wire whisk
Rotary hand beater or electric mixer
Rubber spatulas
*Suribachi* (see p. 126), or mortar and pestle

*Baking and Cooling*

Jelly roll pans or Swiss roll pans
Pastry brushes (to oil pans and brush top of pastries)
Baking sheets, 2 inches smaller than the size of your oven
Loaf pans

Tube pans
Rectangular baking pans with low sides
Rectangular baking trays
Layer cake pans
Springform pans*
Tart tins
Cupcake tins
Assorted tins and molds
Greaseproof paper
Cake racks
Oven thermometer

*Cooking*

Double boiler
Saucepans
Candy thermometer
Flame spreader (metal heat distributor)
Wok, or cast iron pot (for deep-frying)
Oil skimmer

*Decorating*

See p. 51.

*Shaping*

Flute-edge pastry wheel
Cookie cutters
Rolling pin
Pestle (to roll out soft dough)
Pastry cloth
Knife
Baker's scraper (to clean pastry cloth and cut sections of dough)

# Basic Techniques

Everyone has his or her own way of explaining how to beat, sift, fold, mix, and when to boil, bake, steam or fry. Directions will always vary regarding baking terms and

techniques used, as well as ingredients

---

* Springform pans are best because it is easy to remove the cake without disturbing the shape.

called for. The following are some tips that I hope you will find helpful.

Along with these techniques, there is one ingredient that I feel is most essential—*intuition.* For me, baking is an art that I have translated into measurements and step-by-step instructions. I feel that one should come to it with the same enthusiasm and creative spirit that one would bring to any art form, be it painting or writing or making music. What could be more creative than the preparation of food that is both attractive and delicious?

So, please experiment with these recipes, suggestions and methods. Find your own way and bake according to your own good judgment and intuition.

### Beating

Depending upon what you want to accomplish, there are two ways to beat.

1) The first way is to fill the eggs with air. This method uses a rotary hand beater, wire whisk or electric mixer and is mainly used for cake batters.

2) The second type of beating is for mixes that are fairly stiff and already combined. It is best done with a wooden spoon, rotary hand beater or electric mixer. This method is used for eclairs and yeasted pastry.

### Folding

Folding is perhaps the most important technique for working with batters that use only eggs as a leavening agent. It is the gentlest way of combining two or more ingredients to retain the air that you have beaten into them. It should be done with your hand, preferably; or, if you wish, with a rubber spatula.

1) If you are folding in dry ingredients, sift them, then sprinkle them on top of the mixture. If the ingredients are liquid, pour them on slowly, gradually folding them in.

Folding with your hands allows you to feel how light and delicate the mixture really is.

2) Spread your fingers open and cut through the mixture to the bottom of the mixing bowl.

3) Move your hands across the bottom of the bowl and up the side.

4) Bring your hands up, holding some of the batter. Rotate your hands so that you release the mixture.

5) Repeat the whole procedure until all the ingredients are combined but still feel light and delicate.

# Cooking Methods

### Boiling

Boiling in a saucepan over direct heat is a good method for heating up liquids that do not contain any flour.

A double boiler is needed to cook custards, creams or any delicate flour-liquid or egg combination. These may overcook or scorch if left directly on heat.

It is not necessary to stir as often when cooking in a double boiler, but the cooking time must be increased.

### Steaming

This is a very old, but popular method for preparing puddings, pastries, candies and even cakes, allowing the flavors to permeate more evenly through the dessert. When women devoted more time to cooking and baking, they wouldn't think twice about steaming something for 2 to 3 hours.

Oil a coffee can, cake pan or mold. Fill two-thirds full with batter and cover tightly with foil. Place on a rack in a large heavy pot filled with enough boiling water to come one half to three-quarters of the way up the side of the mold.

Cover the pot and steam on a medium-low heat 2 to 3 hours or longer, keeping the water constantly boiling. If the cake is too moist on top after steaming, preheat the oven to 350°F and bake uncovered 10 to 15 minutes to remove excess moisture.

### Deep-frying

(For unrefined oil, see "Preparation of Oil.")

1) Heat oil on a high heat. To test readiness drop a few grains of salt or batter into oil. If salt or batter rises to the top immediately, the oil is ready.

2) Place several pieces of food into tempura pot. Do not overload. This can lower the temperature, making the oil bubble and preventing the batter from cooking properly.

3) Remove pastry when bubbling almost stops.

4) Drain on egg cartons, white paper towels, or unwaxed brown paper bags.

5) Immediately after removing pastry from oil, replace with another piece. If you leave the oil empty, it will burn.

6) Remove excess particles from the oil with an oil skimmer each time before re-using. To reuse oil from fish-frying, cut up a potato or slice of ginger and fry it immediately in the oil before deep-frying the pastry. This will remove the strong fish smell.

### Preparation of oil

(This step is necessary only for unrefined oil or if oil bubbles.)

Place 1 quart oil (one third sesame to two thirds safflower, or all safflower) in a tempura pot or wok. Cook over medium heat until oil begins to move. (If oil is overheated, it will smoke and be unfit for use in cooking.) Turn flame off immediately (or take off heat immediately), and cool.

Unrefined oil often contains naturally occuring liquids which can be boiled off prior to cooking. This accounts for the bubbling often seen when first cooking unrefined oil.

### Baking

Preheat oven to suggested temperature 15 minutes before baking (use an oven thermometer to assure correct temperature).

If the oven is too warm, leave the oven door open for a few minutes to lower the temperature.

Never overload an oven. When both racks are filled, the heat cannot circulate evenly around the pans.

The top rack of an oven is used only for last minute browning. Placing baked goods on the top rack will often result in a browned top and a bottom only half baked.

### Blanching

Sometimes a recipe calls for "blanched nuts," used mainly on the top of a cake for decoration, or for making almond milk. Fresh fruit can also be blanched by the same method.

Drop nuts or fruit into boiling water. Turn off heat and let sit about 1 minute. Drain immediately and rinse under cold water. Peel and use as desired. (If the fruits are organic, save the skins and use them in salads or fruit compotes, or to flavor other desserts.

# Fundamental Foods

### Agar-agar

Agar-agar (also known as *kanten*), a vegetable gelatin made from seaweed, is a rich source of essential minerals. It is used mainly as a thickener, adhesive or emulsifying agent. Having the consistency of gelatin, it will set in a warm or cool spot in approximately half an hour.

It can be purchased in bar form, flakes or powder.

### Amazake

*Amazake* is brewed from sweet brown rice, barley, wheat, or millet. It can be used as a sweetener, drink or leavening agent, depending on how long you let the mixture ferment. It is a delicious substitute for liquor in fruit cakes (before blending), or can be boiled and blended with lemon juice and vanilla as a cream puff or eclair filling.

### Apple Butter

Made from fresh apples which have been cooked down to a soft, butter-like consistency, apple butter can be used as a sweetener or filling.

### Apple Cider (see also Hard Cider)

Cider is the fermented or partially fermented juice of apples. Organic apple cider has no preservatives, so it must be refrigerated at all times to retard natural fermentation.

### Apple Cider Jelly

Apple cider jelly is a concentrated form of apple cider, produced by boiling down the cider until it jells.

### Apple Concentrate

Apple concentrate is made from apples that have been washed and pressed into juice. The juice of the whole apple is cooked over a long period of time. It is so concentrated that 1/4 cup of concentrate will make 2 glasses of apple juice. Although it is known to be a natural sweetener, it is difficult to ensure that the apples it was made from were organically grown.

### Apple Juice

Apples are crushed to a pulp, then pressed to obtain juice. The juice is pasteurized to keep it from fermenting and turning into cider. It may be used in place of any other liquid in any recipe to enhance the flavor.

### Apricot Purée

Boiled down dried fruit.

### Arrowroot

Arrowroot was named by the South American Indians, who used its fresh roots to heal wounds made by poison arrows. Arrowroot is used as a thickening agent in place of flour in many instances, because it does not lose its thickening power when combined with very acid fruits. If overcooked, it has the tendency to lose this good quality.

This thickening agent has properties very similar to those of cornstarch, but it is of better quality. It is a light starch used in glazes, cake batters, doughs, pudding and pie fillings and other dessert mixes. It is very helpful in holding dough together while rolling it out; just sprinkle some on the cloth before you begin to roll. Arrowroot can also be used in food for sick people and children because it is easily digested.

### Barley Malt Extract

Malt is naturally processed by sprouting barley in water. When the sprouts are ready, heat is applied to stop the sprouting and dry out the malt. Use it as a concentrated sweetener in or on any dessert.

### Bean Curd

See Tofu.

### Beet Juice

Boil beets in salted water until soft. Strain off water and use for tinting icings, crusts or cookies.

### Bulgur

To make bulgur, whole wheat is roasted, cracked, parboiled and dried. Bulgur can be used to give a fluffy, light texture to cakes. It is available in natural and Middle Eastern food stores, and can be used in place of couscous.

### Carob

Otherwise known as St. John's Bread, this food is an ideal natural substitute in recipes calling for the use of cocoa or chocolate.

The flavor and color it imparts is similar to that of chocolate, yet without the detrimental effects of oxalic acid, theobromine and caffeine contained in products of the cocoa bean. Available in powdered form, it is sweeter and darker in color than cocoa. See Concentrated Sweeteners (p. 163) for substitution value.

### Corn Sugar

See Molasses.

### Couscous

This is made from the middle of hard semolina wheat which has been precooked before being dried to make it easier to prepare and to give it a lighter, fluffier texture. It is similar to bulgur and is a staple food in the Middle East, and served steamed with other foods and condiments in Tunisia, Morocco and Algeria.

Couscous is available at natural and Middle Eastern food stores and may be used flavored, as a separate dessert, or combined with flour and other ingredients to add lightness to cakes.

### Dried Fruit

Sun-drying is the only natural way to dehydrate food. This drying process evaporates the water from the fruit, so that there is not enough moisture to support bacteria.

The fruits are first picked, washed and peeled, then blanched with steam and spread out on a large tray to dry in the sun. The contact with the air tends to darken the pulp. If the dried fruit you purchase is not darker than the fresh fruit of the same kind, it usually shows that sulfur dioxide was used to preserve the color.

*Eggs*

See Egg Story, p. 30.

*Flour (see also Flour Story, p. 25)*

There are many different types of flour available in natural food stores. It is important to know how they differ from each other, so that you will be able to work successfully with each of them.

*Brown Rice Flour*

This is the most suitable flour to use to achieve a crunchier, sweeter taste and texture.

*Chestnut Flour*

Ground from dried chestnuts, this flour is sweet enough to be used without any additional sweetener, especially if cooked for a long time as a cream (see p. 144), or for toppings or fillings. Chestnut flour can also be used in combination with whole wheat pastry flour in pastry to add crunchiness to pie crusts and cookies, and to lend a distinctive flavor. It is obtainable at natural food and Italian food stores.

If chestnut flour is difficult to obtain, substitute one of the following:
1. 4 parts brown rice flour and 1 part soy flour
2. 4 parts oat flour and 1 part soy flour
3. 4 parts barley flour and 1 part oat flour

*Corn Flour (Maize)*

Made from corn, this flour has a sweet flavor and a delicate quality. It is more finely ground than cornmeal, and is used mainly in fillings.

Corn flour should be used as fresh as possible because it can develop a bitter taste if kept too long.

*Sweet Brown Rice Flour*

This flour is sweeter than brown rice flour, and is best used to make candies, steamed desserts, crunchy cookies or mochi. (The Chinese use sweet rice flour mostly in their desserts, which are usually steamed.)

*Whole Wheat or Whole Meal Flour*

Whole wheat flour is mainly used in breads, although a small amount can be used along with whole wheat pastry flour in yeasted pastries. Because it absorbs more liquid and contains more gluten than whole wheat pastry flour, it can make doughs tough if overworked, but it can also provide a greater rise for certain yeasted products.

*Whole Wheat Pastry Flour*

This flour is made from a different species of wheat, known as soft wheat. It is a low gluten variety of wheat. It may be called cake flour—20 percent whole wheat, 80 percent unbleached white. Some of the best, lightest and most delicious cakes are made from whole wheat pastry flour. Be-

cause it contains the bran from the outside of the wheat kernel, it is slightly brownish in color and a great deal more nutritious than unbleached white flour.

Roasting flour, oats and seeds improves the flavor of desserts and toppings in which they are used. Prepare as follows:

1) Cover the bottom of a dry or oiled heavy skillet or frying pan with the rolled oats, flour or seeds and heat over a low heat.

2) Move the ingredients from side to side, in a clockwise or counterclockwise motion until they are lightly browned and have a strong sweet aroma (when roasting chestnut flour, roast until the flour is a medium shade of brown).

3) Remove from the pan, and place on a plate to cool before using. (Never add warm flour to cool liquid or it will get lumpy.)

Roasting flour adds more flavor, but over roasting can add a bitter taste.

### Grain Coffee (coffee substitute)

Because of the harmful effects caffeine may have on our systems,* more and more people are discovering "grain coffee." This tastes very much like coffee but contains cereals, fruit and roots. It is available in both instant and regular form. The instant is most convenient in dessert making. All recipes when listing grain coffee refer to the instant kind.

When a recipe calls for at least 1/2 cup liquid, regular grain coffee may be substituted for the instant.

To prepare regular grain coffee: Bring liquid to a boil, add grain coffee and perk or simmer 10 minutes. Strain. Substitute for the liquid called for in a recipe.

### Grain Syrup

Grain syrup is a natural sweetener that can be made at home. It can be used as a topping for a cake, or in the same way as maple syrup or honey. Make a large quantity so that you can try it in various ways to see which suits you best.

To prepare, see p. 67.

### Hard Cider (see also Apple Cider)

Hard cider may be made by keeping cider in a loosely closed container at room temperature for two to three days. Leave until the top of the cider is foamy and it has a sharp fermented taste.

### Kanten

See Agar-agar.

### Kuzu

Kuzu (not to be confused with arrowroot) is the powdered root of the wild arrowroot. It is gathered in the high mountains of the Far East. Used medicinally for many years in the Orient, kuzu is traditionally taken as a thick beverage to sooth and strengthen the intestines and other internal organs. It is available at most natural food stores. Kuzu can be used as a thickening agent in place of arrowroot. When substituting, use half the amount of kuzu as arrowroot.

---

* Dr. Irwin Rose wrote in *Science Digest* that caffeine, found in all coffee, has the ability to make your heart beat 15 percent faster, make your lungs work 13 times harder and make your stomach secrete up to 400 percent more hydrochloric acid. Coffee has been linked to ulcers as well as heart disease. Caffeine naturally occurs in coffee beans, cocoa beans, tea leaves and cola nuts.

## Maltose

Maltose is a combination of sprouted wheat and freshly cooked sweet rice. It is allowed to ferment at a high temperature until the starch turns into sugar. At that point, it is cooked, strained and cooled. Highly concentrated and much sweeter in taste than barley malt extract, I recommend it as a sweetener for all types of baking and cooking (see p. 163). Usually found in Chinese or Asian food stores.

## Maple Syrup

Maple trees are native to the north-eastern part of the United States. The Indians used the sweet sap of the tree for making sugar and syrup. The sap of the maple begins to flow usually at the end of February or the beginning of March, and continues for three to four weeks.

The Indians tapped the tree by cutting through the bark and guiding the sap into containers, using curved pieces of bark. The sap was concentrated by dropping hot stones into it, thereby boiling the liquid. Freezing this and removing the ice that formed on top produced sugar.

Today, maple syrup is extracted by drilling holes into the side of the tree and inserting wooden taps to let the sap flow out into buckets.

The sudden change in temperature from a warm day to a freezing night stops the sap from flowing, and the warmth starts it again in the morning.

After the buckets have been filled, the sap is taken to a "sugar house," poured into large containers and cooked over fires, which boil the sap down and concentrate it. It takes 40 gallons of sap (the sap of about 9 maple trees), to make 1 gallon of syrup.

Unfortunately, today many trees are being injected with formaldehyde so that the sap will not coagulate. Formaldehyde not only feeds into the syrup that is sold, but is harmful to the tree, shortening its life by many years.

Syrups are graded A, B and C, depending on the temperature and length of boiling. Grade A Extra Fancy is made from the sweetest sap and has been boiled the longest amount of time. The lighter the color, the better the quality.

Rich in minerals, maple syrup is one of the few naturally occurring sweeteners found today. Because it is so concentrated, it goes a long way. So remember, use maple syrup sparingly (see p. 163).

## Miso

*Miso* is a paste made from fermented soybeans, sea salt, *koji*, water, and sometimes rice or barley. It can be used in the place of sea salt, but mainly it is used as a protein supplement in salad dressings, soups, sauces and sour dough breads. Miso should never be boiled, since boiling destroys the vital emzymes. Simmering reduces its lactic acid content.

For a richer flavor in desserts, try using miso in place of sea salt (1 Tbsp. miso equals 1/2 tsp. sea salt).

## Molasses

There are about four kinds of molasses sold today. "Unsulfured" molasses is said to be made from the juice of the sun-ripened cane. "Sulfured" molasses, believed to be a by-product of refined sugar, picks up sulfur from the fumes used in the process of converting sugar cane into sugar. "Black-strap" molasses, another by-product of the sugar industry, results from boiling down the sugar several times during the refining process. It is the discarded residue of the cane syrup, after the sugar crystals have been extracted.

Sorghum molasses, produced mainly in the United States, is the most pure and least processed of them all. It is the concentrated juice of sorghum, a relative of the millet family, a corn-like cereal grain. The sorghum stems are crushed in a way similar to sugar cane, and boiled to obtain sorghum molasses.

Corn syrup or corn sugar, such as "yellow D" corn sugar, is a product of cornstarch produced by treating corn with sulfuric or hydrochloric acid, then neutralizing and bleaching it with other chemicals. Because it costs less to produce than cane or beet sugar, it is used in tremendous quantities in canned fruits, juices, pastries and other processed foods.

### Mu Tea

*Mu* tea, popular for its strengthening qualities as well as its unusual taste, is a blend of 9 or 16 herbs. It may be served either hot or cold, plain or mixed with apple juice. Because of its delicate flavor, it may be used as a liquid in various desserts, in place of, or in addition to, other spices. It adds zest to pie crusts, pastries, cookies and even cakes. Try substituting it for all or part of the liquid suggested. To prepare, boil 1 bag of mu tea in 4 to 5 cups of water for 20 minutes. You may reuse the bag to make a weaker tea.

### Nut Milk

There are many recipes in other cook books that call for the use of cow's or goat's milk. However, many people have begun to switch over to soy milk and nut milk.

You can make your own nut milk by using any nuts such as almonds, cashews, or sunflower seeds, hot water or apple juice and a blender. Just whip until creamy and smooth.

### Nuts (see also Seed and Nut Butters)

Various kinds of nuts can be used creatively to enhance texture as well as flavor in dessert making.

Shells of walnuts or almonds are sometimes bleached, and shelled nuts sometimes bathed in chemicals to help dissolve the outer skins. But it is possible to find nuts that are organically grown and not adulterated with chemical preservatives.

Roasting imparts a richer taste to any dessert which uses nuts. Purchase nuts without any additives (salt, oil or chemical dyes), and prepare as follows:

Place the nuts on a baking sheet, giving them plenty of room. Preheat the oven 10 minutes at 325°F. Bake nuts, stirring once or twice, until lightly toasted. Over roasting will make them bitter. Store in an airtight glass jar if not to be used immediately.

Nuts that are to be crushed, chopped or ground should be roasted immediately before using. Crushing the nuts releases their oils, enhancing their flavor.

Do not roast nuts too far in advance because they tend to get soggy and stale.

### Oats or Barley

Rolled oats or barley are not just popular as a breakfast cereal. They are used in many cakes, cookies, pie crusts, fillings and toppings as well.

Buy only "rolled oats," or "old-fashioned oats" at the market or natural food store. "Instant oats" or "quick cooking oats" have been heavily processed.

### Oil (see also Oil Story, p. 28)

The best oils for baking and dessert

making are unrefined safflower oil or unrefined corn oil. They are nutritionally rich
and unprocessed, giving a delicate, almost
butter-like effect in cakes, and making the
flakiest pastry dough imaginable. If these oils
are unavailable, the next best oil for desserts
is unrefined sesame oil.

Keep refrigerated after opening.

*Raisin or Sultana Juice*

Blend together 1 cup soaked raisins or
sultanas plus soaking liquid, 1/4 tsp. sea
salt and 1 cup more liquid. If desired, you
may add 1 tsp. of vanilla extract or orange
rind. Can be used in place of fruit juice.

*Raisin or Sultana Purée*

See p. 64.

*Rind*

Fresh rind is the freshly grated skin of
an orange, tangerine or lemon.

I searched many natural food stores for
organic flavorings in the form of dried
orange, tangerine or lemon rind when I
began to bake commercially. The only rind
available was colored, sugared and chemically treated, so I had to make my own. Here
is a quick and easy method for making your
own rind. Made this way, rind can be
stored indefinitely, so make extra.

1) Slice an organic fruit into quarters.
2) Peel off the skin and discard the white
pulp beneath the skin (this white is very
bitter and should not be used).
3) Dry the skin outside in the sun on a
bamboo mat so that the air circulates all
round. It will become hard and dry.
4) Blend the skin in a blender 3 to 5
minutes until it turns into a fine powder.
5) Store in a tightly sealed container in
a cool, dark place.

6) If you do not have a blender, grate
the rind on the smallest side of a grater.
Use fresh or dry and store as above.

*Rolled Oats or Barley*

See Oats.

*Salt*

See Salt Story, p. 29.

*Seed and Nut Butters (see also Tahini)*

Seed or nut butters are made by grinding
roasted or unroasted seeds or nuts to a
creamy texture. The most commonly used
are peanut butter, almond butter and sesame
butter.

Unlike tahini, which is made from hulled
sesame seeds, sesame butter is made from
whole, roasted sesame seeds. Substituting
one seed or nut butter for another can
enhance flavor and add variety in texture to
your desserts.

*Seeds*

Sesame seeds not only provide us with
sesame oil, sesame butter and tahini, but
also lend a decorative effect to glazes and
any pastries, as well as a crunchy texture to
cookies. They are a rich source of calcium
and protein. Sesame seeds should be lightly
roasted before using.

Sunflower, poppy and pumpkin seeds are
also rich in oil and delicious in cookies,
cakes, breads, candies and pastries. They
make a fine snack that is rich in vitamin E,
and can lend an attractive finished as well.
Sunflower and poppy seeds, too, should be
lightly roasted before using to aid digestion.

### Soy Milk

Increasing in popularity in the West, it has been a staple food for many hundreds of years among Asian people. Rich in protein, low in fat, it has served as the backbone of most eastern diets as a daily source of protein. See p. 159.

### Tahini

*Tahini* is made from hulled sesame seeds which have been lightly toasted to preserve their inherent nutritional value. Tahini that appears loose and liquidly may have been adulterated with poor quality oil and chemicals.

Tahini contains lecithin, phosphorus, calcium, iron and vitamins B and E, and is abundantly supplied with protein.

It can be used to make a delicious malted recipe and can be blended with oatmeal, raisins and vanilla, to be used as a milk substitute, or spread on bread or crackers. It is used in baking as a flavoring, filling, icing or sauce.

Fresh tahini has a creamy consistency. If tightly covered and stored in a cool place, it should keep for many months.

### Tofu (Soybean Cheese)

*Tofu* (pronounced "dofu" in Chinese) can be purchased at most natural, Asian or Oriental food stores. It is made from soybeans by soaking, grinding and boiling. Then it is strained through a fine cloth bag, separating the outside of the bean from the milk. To this liquid (soy milk), lemon juice, calcium sulfate (gypsum), vinegar or natural *nigari* (seawater extract) is added. The liquid is covered and set aside for several minutes. The whey is removed and the tofu is placed into settling boxes which have holes to allow the excess whey to drain off. It is pressed until a solid block is formed. It is then cut under water and allowed to soak 1 hour before being packaged.

Tofu is high in protein, and low in calories and fats. It is used daily in the Orient as a staple form of low cost protein. Its light, delicate texture embellishes any dessert as a cream, filling, or custard. It has the ability to adapt to a creamy consistency and can jell into any shape or form without a binding agent.

Remember to keep tofu covered with water and refrigerate until using. Change the water when cloudy.

### Vanilla Essence or Extract

Vanilla is a natural flavor found in the form of a bean or liquid. Most of the vanilla available in supermarkets today is artificially produced with chemicals and boosted with vanillin, which is made from a coal derivative.

There are two different "natural" vanillas available: vanilla essence and vanilla extract. These differ only in the way that they are made. Vanilla essence is made by an extraction method that first soaks the bean in an alcohol base solution, then drains off the liquid and adds caramel coloring to it (to stabilize the color because each batch can come out looking different).

The second process begins by boiling down vanilla beans with water. The same coloring is then added to the mixture to standardize it. This is known as vanilla extract.

If pure vanilla extract is unavailable, substitute a bean for the liquid and prepare as follows:

Soak the bean in the cooking liquid until soft. Simmer at least 15 minutes. (The longer the soaking or simmering, the more flavor will be added to the liquid. If you do not have time for the long soaking or simmering, you may omit this step. Cooking will also help to bring out the vanilla flavor.)

Remove the bean and use the liquid. Dry the bean and reuse it again.

If neither bean nor extract is available, substitute grated orange or lemon rind in equal proportions, or to taste.

*Yeast*

See p. 104.

# Natural Needs

The natural sweetness and fragrance of freshly pressed, organic apple cider, the strong rich taste and texture of whole grains ground into flour, the clear golden color and distinct aroma of unrefined oil, and the natural color and flavor of the sea's greatest gift to man, salt—these are the basic tools of my art.

I would like to share with you what I have learned about the different qualities of basic ingredients, and why I chose certain natural, organic ingredients over refined ones.

## Flour Story

In prehistoric times, flour was milled by the pounding of grains between two stones. In time, the lower stone became hollowed out and the upper one rounded, making the mortar and pestle or saddlestone. About 300 B.C., the rotary mill (so-called) quern was developed. This mill enabled the grain to be poured down through a hole in the upper stone, slowly feeding down to a lower stone and a stick. This stick, serving as a lever, turned the upper stone against the lower. Slaves or strong animals turned the larger mill stones to grind the grain into fresh flour or meal.

A hundred years ago, our grandparents and great grandparents made their own breads, cakes, cookies, pastries, pies and puddings using freshly ground whole wheat or other whole grain flours. The bread we eat today is no longer the "staff of life" which nourished and sustained our grandparents. It is largely made from "refined" white flour, either bleached or bromated or both.

In the past century, commercial flour has been stripped more and more of natural vitamins and minerals. To begin with, most wheat today is grown with chemical fertilizers, pesticides or herbicides. These lower the protein content. Then, in the refining process, the outer coating, or bran of the wheat, is removed and the flour is usually bleached by chlorine gas to make it "white." The outer bran is the part of the grain which contains most of the proteins, minerals and vitamins. It is one of the richest sources of vitamin B and E. This coating, which also provides roughage or lubrication for the intestinal tract, is broken up in the milling of the whole wheat flour. Thus, the digestion of foods made with this flour is actually more difficult than that of unmilled whole grains.

Moreover, the grinding itself exposes the grain to oxidation which quickly destroys a great deal of nutritional value. Finally, commercial processes to make the flour store longer (have a longer shelf life) destroy almost all of the wheat, or add chemicals which are easily absorbed by the starches inside the kernel. In this way, flour can be stored for years at any temperature and shipped to all parts of the world with never a rancid taste to spoil it. Synthetic vitamins and minerals are added not to "enrich," but actually to restore some of the nutrients that would ordinarily be present in the whole grain. No wonder bread and other flour products sold today all have the word "enriched" on the label, for almost all the valuable natural nutrients have been removed.

During the First World War, a doctor by the name of Sir William Wilcox discovered that an epidemic of beriberi (an extreme deficiency of vitamin B) which had been destroying the British troops in India, did not effect the Indians. Sir William found that the Indian troops had been fed their native stone-ground whole wheat flour, while the British troops had been fed a white flour.

Flour is available in many different qualities, each one used for a specific purpose. I suggest that you buy whole grains if possible, and that you grind your own in a grain mill (obtainable in natural food stores), to secure the least amount of nutritional loss. If you cannot grind your own grain, the next best thing to do is to buy your flour no more than a day before baking. Choose a reputable natural food store that receives fresh shipments once or twice a week.

If flour is allowed to sit on the shelf more than 10 days after milling, it may lose all nutrients. Since it is usually necessary to keep flour at least several days after it has been milled, be sure that the store, as well as you, keeps it refrigerated and away from light. A cold temperature does not eliminate nutritional loss completely, but if does slow it down considerably.

## Sugar Story

The true meaning of the phrase "white sugar" came to me one day when a friend served me honey for my tea instead of sugar. She explained that she had stopped using sugar when she found out that all commercially packaged sugar was without nutritional value and even harmful to the body. Giving me some literature to read on the subject, she emphasized that sugar, "white" or "natural raw," was grown and processed in the same way. Synthetic fertilizers and weed sprays were applied to the growing plants, and when harvested they were put through cleaning, decolorizing, purifying, sterilizing, crystallizing and drying processes. Reading and listening to her, I began to see that by the time it reaches us, sugar has been stripped of all its natural vitamins and minerals and become truly valueless as a food.

Our grandparents were led to believe that "raw" sugar was inferior to the refined, white product because it was dark and full of impurities. Actually the reverse was true: the dark vibrant color was proof of the presence of natural minerals. But in 1898, certain sugar refiners procured a chemist that was willing to say that upon examination "raw" sugar was found to contain "disease producing insects." It was then proposed that only refined sugar be sold because "those terrible creatures" do not occur in refined sugar of any quality, and a law prohibiting the sale of unrefined sugar in this country was passed. Today, "raw," and even "brown" sugar is made by processing white sugar one step further— putting molasses back into it for color and flavor. Sugar is heated in the presence of lime which eliminates the calcium salts and destroys almost all of the vitamins. Then it is put into contact with lime, carbonate of soda, carbonic acid and sulfurous anhydride and cooked several times, cooled, crystallized, and put into a centrifuge. The remaining molasses is then treated with strontium hydroxide in order to extract the remaining sugar. Then the sugar is purified with carbonic calcium acid, bleached, filtered through charred animal bones and dyed with a coloring derived from tar.

Refined sugar of whatever color is highly touted as an energy food, but this is another misconception. According to Dr McCracken of the University of California, pure or almost pure sugar (sucrose) such as refined sugar is the worst of all foods. It is absorbed so rapidly into the body through the bloodstream that it may trigger an over production of insulin; this reduces the blood sugar to harmfully low levels, a condition known as hypoglycemia. However, sugar obtained from natural foods, such as grains and vegetables, is absorbed into the bloodstream gradually and does not upset the delicate balance of high and low blood sugar levels. Thus it gives the body more energy to work with.

The amount of sugar primitive people could eat was limited by the amount of food from natural sources their stomachs and intestines could hold. When they ate sugar they also were eating protein, vitamins, minerals and other valuable foods along with it. Because their sugar supply came mainly from natural fruits and vegetables, their body was able to break down the sugar into glucose gradually without straining.

Today, we eat pound after pound of refined sugar without being restrained by any natural fiber. Not getting any nutrients with it, especially those which are necessary to help metabolize the sugar, we strain our pancreas and other internal organs by eating sugar in the form of sucrose. The stress of bypassing the natural digestive process of breaking sugar down into glucose causes undue strain on the body and can lead eventually to severe illness.

A number of other ill effects can be produced in the body by sugar. Dr. Dennis P. Burkitt of the Medical Research Council of London has stated that refined sugar alters the bacteria in the lining of the intestines. Such altered bacteria are capable of breaking down bile salts to form cancer-producing material. Dr. Burkitt said, "You can put the whole thing down to food—especially white flour and sugar."

There is ample evidence to prove that refined sugar encourages bacteria to eat up B vitamins and kills certain bacteria that help produce vitamins and enzymes in the body. In order to digest sugar (which has lost its own vitamins during the refining process), the body must take vitamin B and minerals such as calcium from the heart, liver, kidneys and nervous system, resulting in other deficiencies as well. The instant energy or "sugar rush" occurring immediately upon sugar entering the system paralizes the stomach until acids are mobilized to neutralize it. This overproduction of acids is counteracted by an emergency mobilization of stored minerals. Calcium is the first mineral to be used and is therefore the most easily depleted mineral in the body.

Furthermore, when we have an excess of sugar in our bodies, the liver stores it. When the liver is overloaded, it returns the excess sugar to the blood in the form of fatty acids. These get circulated throughout the body. They are stored as accumulated solid fat in the thighs, buttocks and other less active areas, and can cause the heart to become sluggish and perhaps even to stop. Thus even though sugar is not fat it can *change* into fats when taken excessively.

Other symptoms have been related to the over consumption of sugar. These include loss of appetite, fatigue, tooth decay, depression, difficulty in thinking, rheumatism due to a calcium-phosphorus imbalance and even mental illness. Refined sugar irritates the mucous membranes, blood vessels, glands and digestive organs because it is unnaturally concentrated.

To me, it is senseless to try to use "better" sugar; when, in effect, it is all the same. I strongly recommend that sugar be eliminated entirely from the diet. Choose instead a natural sweetener such as sun dried fruits, barley malt extract, ame (rice honey), maltose, apple juice, maple syrup, molasses, fruit concentrates (e.g. apples), or on rare occasions, honey. (Of course too much of any thing, including natural sugars, may also be harmful to the body.) Carrots, beets, parsnips and other vegetables, fruits and grains contain many valuable nutrients as well as natural sugars. We do not need added sugar to satisfy our daily requirements because our bodies convert more than half of our food into blood sugar. So bake with natural ingredients. They will make your desserts taste better and your family and friends feel better.

# Oil Story

Oils are usually obtained from seeds, flowers, beans, and the kernels of native and tropical fruits and grain. Seeds constitute one of the most important sources of man's food supply, because within their structures are the elements and properties essential to the beginning and reproduction of life. Most of the oils we use are pressed from oil-bearing seeds such as safflower, sesame, sunflower, soybean, and the germ of whole corn kernel.

It seems that one of the chief aims of the food processing industry is to make the food look "pure." Food processors remove valuable nutrients, which give natural color, odor and flavor, in an effort to make foods look whiter, brighter, lighter and clearer. Oil is no exception.

Most of the cooking oils commonly sold today are refined so much that they are usually flat tasting, odorless and dull-looking, but according to the manufacturer, they are "pure." The refining process subjects oil to heating, the addition of acids, bleaching and the alteration of extreme hot and cold temperatures. These treatments are not without their ill-effects.*

---

* Dr Roger Williams in his book, called *Nutrition Against Disease*, outlines the dangers of refined oils. In tests which compared refined oils in relation to unrefined oils, it was shown that refined oils actually increased the cholesterol levels in the blood and increased the danger of heart disease. Refined oils are sold under nationally known brands labeled as cold-pressed. These can be easily distinguished by their light color, and lack of odor and taste. In his book, Dr Williams suggested that all consumers take the extra time and trouble to seek out unrefined and pressed oils, and that the threat to health posed by these refined oils was too great to be overlooked.

Unrefined oils, on the other hand, still contain original substances which give natural color, odor and flavor not usually present in a refined oil. As a consumer, you can tell if an oil is truly unrefined and pure by using your senses. An oil that has not been chemically refined will be darker, thicker, and have an odor and flavor similar to the source from which it was pressed.

It was a pleasant surprise to discover oils that were not bland, tasteless or odorless, and that could be used for cooking as well as baking. Nutritious and flavorful, these unrefined oils provide vitamins A, E and K along with lecithin, which helps to break down cholesterol deposits in the tissues of the body.

Saturated fats are mainly responsible for cholesterol deposits that form in the tissues, clogging the arteries and the veins. One way to distinguish between saturated and unsaturated fats is by observing them at room temperature: the saturated fats are solid, but the harmless unsaturated fats are usually liquids, otherwise known as oils.

I recommend that you use good-quality, unrefined oils, such as corn, corn-germ, safflower, sesame, soybean or olive when cooking and baking instead of refined oils, like butter, margarine or shortening. You will be amazed at the difference in taste, texture and aroma of your products, and, at the same time, at the improved health of the persons who enjoy them.

Store your oils in a cool place to assure their freshness.

## Salt Story

Salt has always been one of the most common and important ingredients of life. Thousands of years ago, it was the only preservative used by man. At one time it had religious significance, for it was the symbol of purity among the ancient Hebrews, who rubbed newborn babies with it to ensure their good health. The Old Testament tells the story of Elisha throwing salt into a spring to purify its waters (2 Kings, 2:19–22). In the Near East, salt used at meals is a sign of friendship and hospitality. The Arabs say, "There is salt between us," meaning we have eaten together and are friends. Salt was once so precious that Caesar's soldiers received part of their pay for the purpose of buying common salt; it was known as their *salarium*, which is where our word *salary* comes from. From ancient times through the Renaissance, some of Europe's important highways were salt trade routes. Even before the Romans, the Celts would carry salt from western Austria to the Baltic Sea, where they would exchange it for amber.

All salt was at one time essentially sea salt. Today, there are three main kinds of salt on the market: unrefined sun-dried sea salt, iodized salt, and refined table salt. Salt found inland, in rock deposits or in springs that flow through them, can be traced back to the ocean that covered the earth millions of years ago. Earth movements isolated parts of this ancient sea, which evaporated, uncovering these beds of rock.

Unrefined, sun-dried, white sea salt contains many minerals that are not found in refined table salt: gold, iron, copper, calcium, and magnesium which are important to our digestive processes, are present in small quantities.

In ancient times, people kept crude, gray sea salt in a jar for at least one year. During that time, the magnesium absorbed water from the air and went to the bottom of the jar. The top salt became less salty and purer, and was used in cooking and baking. Usually this salt was roasted to make it drier and ground into a fine powder before it was used.

Most salt found in the stores today has had the trace minerals removed, supposedly to make it taste "saltier" and look purer. The refining process subjects salt to great pressure and steam heat, causing it to crystallize instantly. Although this method saves money, the crystal produced is not only devoid of its trace minerals but also slow to dissolve and difficult to digest.

Try this experiment to see if your salt has been refined. Place a teaspoon of salt in a glass of water and stir it once. Look at it a little while later to see if there is any sediment. Natural, unrefined sea salt has a tendency to disappear in the water within a few minutes, leaving the liquid clear (a residue or cloudiness in the water may indicate the presence of impurities), but the refined table salt will take longer to dissolve.

Commercial table salt may also contain additives. Calcium bicarbonate is added to keep it dry and pourable, and iodine, which is commonly used to prevent goiter,* may also be added. Dextrose, a simple sugar, is added to stabilize the iodine, because it is very volatile and oxidizes in direct sunlight. Other additives are used to keep the salt looking white.

It is important to use salt that is as pure and unrefined as nature intended it, salt that has not been treated with chemical additives, but has been extracted from the sea and allowed to dry naturally in the sun. Therefore, when you buy salt, remember that while it may be the smallest ingredient you use in quantity, it is just as important, or even more important, than the other ingredients in your cooking and baking. It can bring out the delicate flavors of other ingredients, sometimes actually making them sweeter.

# Egg Story

Eggs are prepared by nature to serve as food for the growing, unborn bird. They contain all the minerals and vitamins essential to support life. Thus they can be good food for humans too, if not taken to excess. But the quality of the eggs we use depends upon the food we feed the hen and the environment in which she lives.

Commercial chickens are usually raised to yield the greatest amount of eggs or meat, disregarding the natural environment and diet of the birds. Stimulants are used to increase the productivity of the chickens. Amphetamines and arsenic are sometimes put into their feed to increase their appetite so that they will weigh more and draw a better price at the marketplace. These additives result in large chemical deposits in commercial eggs and chicken meat. Furthermore, the meat and fish-meal fed to these chickens are of the lowest possible quality and full of preservatives, hormones and weight-gaining stimulants as well. Other unnatural ingredients in commercial eggs include antibiotics, phosphates and meat steroids.

The best eggs to buy are those marked: organic and fertile, free or open range. This indicates that the birds that laid the eggs have been fed high-quality food without additives or preservatives, and that the eggs are complete and whole. These eggs have many natural growth-promoting hormones which can be lacking in sterile, nonorganic eggs.

Hens produce richer, more nutritious eggs if they are allowed to run freely on the ground in uncluttered pens, and to mate

---

* Iodine is naturally supplied by the following, in order of highest iodine content: kelp, agar-agar, swiss chard, turnip greens, summer squash, mustard greens, watermelon, cucumber, spinach.

freely. Healthier and happier chickens, and eggs with more vitality, can produce healthier and happier people.

## Milk Story

Milk is a transitionary food that is secreted by female mammals to help their offspring adjust from the womb to the outside world. Cow's milk, which is richer in protein, fats and minerals than human milk, helps to build the strong bones essential for calves. However, humans first develop a strong nervous system which is aided by human milk because of its rich, easily digestible fats, more digestible protein and more alkaline factors.

No other mammal uses milk after infancy. The arrival of teeth transforms infants from a liquid to a solid state eating mammal—time to forget about drinking milk. In fact, we tend to loose the ability to digest milk as we grow older. About 80 percent of the adults in the world lack the enzyme *lactase* needed to digest lactose (sugar in milk). Undigested milk has been known to form mucus which can clog the system and cause disease.

Milk, both cow's and goat's, were traditionally consumed when people were nomadic with no fixed crops to live on and needed food that was rich in saturated fats to keep warm. However, the amount of milk, butter and cheese consumed was very small in comparison with today. The consumption of dairy foods in the last fifty years has just about doubled, but the quality of our dairy products today is very different. Cattle are not allowed to live a natural existence mainly because of economic reasons. The residues of chemical sprays and pesticides, and the hormones that are fed to cattle to fatten them and stimulate milk production, are all passed into the milk of the cow in a more concentrated form. The lack of exercise and restricted diet of the modern cow has changed the balance of the fats in their milk and meat.

## Baking Soda and Baking Powder

Both of these common leavening agents have been used for a great number of years. Sometimes these leavening agents have proved detrimental to people's health.

Many natural food stores have begun to carry a range of different kinds of low-sodium baking powder that contain no lime or aluminum compounds. However, these still can have an adverse reaction in some people.

Baking soda is not recommended at all because it has been known to cause extreme inflammation of the stomach and severe cramps. The best advice I can give is to use sour dough starters for bread and occasionally yeast and/or eggs for cakes on special occasions.

# 2. LAYER AFTER LAYER: *Cakes for All Occasions*

Creating new dessert recipes is one of my greatest pleasures. Whether the occasion is a special party, a friend's birthday, a wedding celebration or a request to supply cakes to a natural food store or restaurant, I use it as a reason to experiment.

Here are some suggestions that I would like to share with you. They can alter consistency, texture and taste of cakes. I hope that through these hints you can develop special techniques that work for you, so that you may create and embellish imaginative recipes on your own.

## Leavening

Most of these cake recipes rely on eggs and/ or yeast for lightness in texture. Because the flour that is used has not been pre-sifted, bleached, bromated or stripped of all the bran, it reacts differently with other ingredients. Most of the cakes will not rise 3 to 4 inches; they will be lower than the normal "layer cake." If you wish a higher cake, bake several layers instead of one or two, increase the amount of yeast suggested by half, or double the amount of eggs.

*Eggs*

Fresh eggs have a tiny air space in between the lining and the shell at either end. A fresh egg will sink in water, end down, and a less fresh egg will float on its side.

In all recipes, eggs should be used at room temperature. If they are cold, they should be warmed as follows: Combine eggs and sweetener in a mixing bowl. Stir for 1 minute. Set the bowl over a pan of hot water on low heat until contents are lukewarm. Stir occasionally to prevent them from cooking or sticking to the pan. Take off heat.

To use whole eggs in baking a cake, beat with a rotary beater, wire whisk or electric mixer until the eggs have almost doubled in volume, and are thick, fluffy and filled with air. Do not overmix when folding in with other ingredients, or you will force the air out of the eggs, and the result will be a heavy cake.

*Separated Eggs*

If you separate the eggs, the batter will usually be lighter.

Crack the egg and let white fall into a mixing bowl, catching yolk on half of shell. Transfer yolk to other half of shell, alternating back and forth, letting remainder of white fall from shell into bowl.

Place yolk in a separate bowl. Mix with a fork and add the other ingredients called for.

Begin to mix whites and sea salt together slowly, until whites become foamy (use rotary beater, wire whisk or electric beater). Increase the motion and beat without stopping until whites look airy and stand up in firm peaks.

Fold whites into batter by hand (p. 15), or with a rubber spatula, to retain as much air as possible.

Bake batter as quickly as possible without banging or opening the door until at least half of the baking time suggested has elapsed.

*Yeast*

See p. 103 "Higher and Higher" for instruction in using yeast in baking.

*Moisture*

Sometimes home ovens (gas or electric) tend to be too dry for certain batters. Those batters that do not have any leavening agents at all may form a hard crust on top of the cake before it is sufficiently baked on the inside. To prevent this, place a small pan of hot water in the bottom of the oven while baking unyeasted, eggless batters. This allows more moisture in the air to circulate around the pans and prevents a crust from forming. This method may also be used when baking yeasted batters, but allow more baking time.

**Alternate Method**
Cover baking pan and steam for half of the recommended baking time (use a cover that is high enough to allow for rising). Remove cover and bake until cake is done.

# Sweetening

Most of the recipes call for a minimum amount of sweetener, allowing the flavor and taste of the other ingredients to come through. However, you may want to use more sweetener than is suggested for some occasions.

Add as much concentrated sweetener (maple syrup, fruit concentrates, grain honey, molasses, barley malt, maltose) as you like, or supplement with apple butter, apple cider jelly, amasake, grain syrup or fruit purée, decreasing the amount of liquid proportionately. Oil cup before measuring. (See Sweetness Equivalency Chart, p. 163.)

Experimenting with different qualities and quantities of sweeteners allows you the flexibility needed in creating your own imaginative recipes.

# Ready or Not

Insert a thin wire cake-tester or metal skewer into the center of the cake. It will come out dry when the cake is ready.

Press a fingertip lightly in the center of the cake. The center will spring back when the cake is done.

A leavened cake will pull away from sides of pan when baked.

# Removing Cakes from Pan

Run a knife around the edge of the cake. Place a cake rack on top of the cake in its pan. Invert rack, pan and cake simultaneously. Let stand until the cake begins to contract away from the sides of the pan. If cake does not begin to slip down out of the pan and onto the rack, take a cold damp sponge and run it over the bottom of the pan several times. Then with the handle of a wooden spoon, tap the bottom of the pan gently, in a circular motion, until the cake begins to fall.

Egg cakes should be left to cool in the turned off oven with the door ajar. This helps prevent cake from falling.

If you are using a baba form (pan with a hole in the center), set the tube on the neck of a bottle so that air can circulate around it while cooling.

When using a springform pan, place it on a cake rack and let stand until cake begins to contract away from the side of the pan. Run a knife around the side of the pan, unclip and remove the side. Allow to cool before removing the bottom.

# Forget Me Knots

1. Liquid content will vary according to the temperature of the room, the moisture in the flour and the air, and the general weather conditions of the day.
2. Preheat the oven 15 minutes before baking, using a temperature gauge inside the oven. An overheated oven may produce a cracked, heavy cake, and an underheated oven will produce a soggy cake.
3. Use all ingredients at room temperature so that they will blend more evenly and easily.
4. Unless otherwise specified, the best oils to use for all baking are unrefined corn-germ oil, corn, sesame or safflower oil. Too much oil may cause the cake to be too crumbly to handle.
5. Sift flour before measuring, never shaking the flour down into the cup after sifting; sift only to get out the lumps. Do not separate the bran from the wheat except for very delicate cakes or pastries. Add the bran back to the sifted flour (or reserve for puddings, breads), before folding it into the batter.
6. Too much flour (or too little liquid) will make the cake uneven and dry.
7. Bulgur wheat or couscous adds lightness to unleavened cakes.
8. When adding eggs to an eggless recipe, decrease the amount of liquid accordingly (1 egg=1/5 cup liquid).
9. When using fewer eggs than called for, substitute 1 tsp. arrowroot or 2 tsp. whole wheat pastry flour for each omitted egg.
10. Use 1/2 tsp. lemon juice to every 3 egg whites to make a stiffer white, with larger volume and greater stability.
11. When measuring liquid sweeteners, oil the measuring cup to prevent the sticky liquid from adhering to the cup.
12. Wooden utensils are preferable because metal can alter the taste.
13. When using a hand beater, extra time should be allotted for beating.
14. Overbeating will break down air bubbles after they have been formed, leaving a heavy, dry cake (yeasted batters excluded).
15. To prevent cake from sticking to the bottom of the pan, dust a little flour over the oiled pan.
16. When placing batters containing eggs in a pan, *do not pat down* batter or bang pan; this motion will cause the air in the eggs to escape.
17. When a cake sticks to a pan, wrap a damp cloth around the pan for a few minutes, and it should come out more easily.
18. To keep a cake from drying up, drop an apple or orange in the cake box, and keep it in a cool place.
19. An old-fashioned way to preserve fruit cake up to one year is as follows: Pour 1 teaspoonful of brandy over the underside of the cake, and let it soak. Wrap it up in a clean cloth which has been sprinkled with brandy. Place it in an earthenware crock with a tight lid; lay a fresh apple on top of the cake, and cover. Once a week, set the crock on a range until it is warmed, taking out the apple before warming. Place a fresh apple in the crock every 2 weeks and renew the brandy application as well. (Hard cider may be substituted for brandy.)

# Recipes

At the end of a meal, when the appetite is usually more than satisfied the surprise dessert awakens an unknown desire for a little bit more. Cakes usually reserved for special occasions such as birthdays, weddings or anniversaries, can be used most any time for any occasion. It's the icing or glaze that can adapt the dessert to any kind of meal. Any leftover cake, can be redressed and served the following day or cooked up into a delightful fruit pudding.

Whatever the reason, you will find a cake for all of them and may even bake a cake and then look for an excuse to serve it!

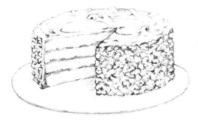

## Basic Cake

> 1/2 cup concentrated sweetener (p. 163)
> 6 egg yolks
> 1/2 cup unrefined safflower or corn oil
> 1 cup date purée (p. 64)
> 2 cups sifted whole wheat pastry flour
> 2 tsp. cinnamon
> 1 tsp. ground coriander
> 1/2 cup roasted crushed almonds
> 2 tsp. lemon rind
> 1/2 tsp. sea salt
> 6 egg whites
> Pinch of sea salt
> 1 tsp. almond essence

Beat sweetener and yolks together until the mixture looks like thick cream. Slowly drip in the oil and continue beating until fully absorbed. Stir in date purée until smooth.

Sift together next three ingredients. Add almonds, rind and salt, and fold into first mixture.

Beat egg whites with pinch of sea salt till stiff peaks form. Gently fold about 1/3 of the egg whites into the batter and then add the remaining whites to batter, folding gently. Add almond essence. Preheat oven to 350°F.

Bake in oiled and floured cake tins for 60 minutes or until cake tests done. Turn off oven and leave door slightly ajar. Leave cake there until cool. Remove from pan when cool and ice.

## Chestnut Icing

> 1 cup tahini or any nut butter
> 1 cup Chestnut Cream (p. 144)
> 1/4 cup concentrated sweetener
> 1 Tbsp. grated orange rind
> 2–3 Tbsp. carob powder
> 1 tsp. *shoyu*
> 2 tsp. vanilla

Blend all ingredients together slowly, adding hot water or apple juice until desired consistency is reached.

*Marzipan*

To make a marzipan that you can roll out, do not add too much liquid. (It may not be necessary to add any at all.) Roll out on greaseproof paper to desired thickness and size. Place on top of cake, then cream the rest of the chestnut icing with hot liquid and pipe it around the sides of the cake. Press almonds around top.

### Variations

*Tofu Sour Cream*
Combine Tofu Sour Cream I (p. 147), 1/2

cup apples and 1/2 tsp. cinnamon or ginger. Spoon this topping over the cake 10 minutes before the cake is done. Lower temperature to 300°F and bake until browned.

*Vanilla Icing*

Increase vanilla to 2 Tbsp.

*Special Party Cake*

Add to basic recipe 3 eggs and 1/4 to 1/2 cup more flour. This will yield a larger cake or 2 smaller ones.

*Tangerine, Orange or Lemon*

Add 2 tsp. more of tangerine, orange or lemon rind, and 3 Tbsp. juice of fruit; or add juice and rind of half a grated orange, lemon or tangerine.

*Seed*

Add 2 Tbsp. caraway, roasted poppy, sunflower or sesame seeds before folding in flour.

*Nut*

Add 1/2 cup roasted chopped nuts— almonds, walnuts, pecans or cashews— before folding in flour. Or prepare 1/2 cup cooked chestnuts (pp. 144 and 145). Add to mixture before folding in flour.

*Dried Fruit*

Marinate 1/4 cup dried fruit in apple juice or cider to cover overnight. Squeeze out liquid; dice fruit and add before folding in a small amount of flour.

*Spice*

Sift into the flour before adding to egg mixture 2 tsp. cinnamon or dried mint, 1/4 tsp. cloves, 1/2 tsp. ginger; *or* 1 tsp. cloves, 1 tsp cinnamon.

*Ginger*

Sift into flour before adding to egg mixture 2 tsp. cinnamon, 1/4 tsp. cloves, 1 tsp. ginger.

*Coffee*

Mix 4 Tbsp. instant grain coffee (p. 20) with the yolks. Or add 1/2 cup instant grain coffee to dry ingredients before folding into eggs.

## Sour Cream Coffee Cake

Follow recipe for Basic Cake (p. 37). Combine 1 cup Tofu Sour Cream (p. 147) and 1 to 2 Tbsp. extra sweetener. Add this to eggs or egg yolks in basic recipe. Also add 1/2 cup instant grain coffee (p. 20) and 1/4 cup additional whole wheat pastry flour to dry ingredients before folding into egg mixture.

**Alternate Method**

1. Follow recipe for Basic Cake (p. 37), adding 1–2 Tbsp. extra sweetener and 1/2 cup instant grain coffee to dry ingredients before folding in eggs. Prepare 1 cup Tofu Sour Cream and spoon on top of cake 10 minutes before baking time has elapsed.
2. Prepare 1 cup Crumb Topping (p. 66). Follow recipe for Basic Cake. Add grain coffee and sweetener as in alternate method above. Pour half of the batter into pan, sprinkle half of topping over it and cover it with remaining batter. Spoon Tofu Sour Cream on top of cake and sprinkle remaining Crumb Topping over it 10 minutes before baking time has elapsed.

## Petit Fours

Petit fours, or "little cakes," are made by cutting large Basic Cakes into smaller, different-shaped cakes—diamond, square, round, triangular or rectangular. They are very delightful to serve at children's parties or as small dessert cakes for unexpected guests. It is a great way to "dress up" leftovers and serve as a new dessert to friends and family. For example:

METHOD A

1. Cut cake into thirds.
2. Cut one part into eight squares.
3. Cut another section into small rectangles.

4. Cut remaining third into triangles and diamonds by cutting diagonally in strips, then cut again diagonally.
5. Dip squares into glaze (p. 61), sprinkle crushed nuts on top.
6. Spread Icing (p. 60) on top of rectangles.
7. Decorate with raisins (features of a face), orange, tangerine or lemon rind, crushed roasted nuts, seeds, mint.
8. Spread cream (p. 146) on top and sides of diamonds and trim the edges with seeds or crushed nuts.
9. Spread with Tofu Cream (p. 147).

METHOD B
1. Cut cake into 1/4-inch slices.
2. Spread five slices with Fruit Purée (p. 64).
3. Stack six slices to make six layers.
4. Cut into 1-inch slices and then cut slices into 2-inch cubes.
5. Top with any crushed, roasted nut, seed, lemon, orange, or tangerine rind or shredded coconut.

## Birthday Cakes

Bake any cake. Cut each layer into two. Spread any thick icing or filling between layers and all around the sides. Roll the sides of the cake in roasted crushed nuts. Spoon glaze over top.

## Cupcakes

Use any cake recipe. Fill oiled cupcake tin half full with cake batter.
Put 1 Tbsp. fruit purée, cream or custard in center. Cover with remaining batter and bake.

## Cupcakes Surprise

Bake cupcakes. Cool and cut a thin slice off the top.
Scoop out the center and fill with custard, cream or purée. Replace the top, glaze, and serve.

**Cloves (***Eugenia caryophyllata***)**
Cloves are produced from a tree that is native to Indonesia. They are the dried flower buds of the tree. The trees, which grow to about 40 feet in height, begin to bear at about 8 or 9 years old, and have a life span of about 60 years. The buds are picked by hand and dried in the sun for several days. Clove is mainly used as a spice for cakes, cookies, pies and pastry.

## Boston Fruit Cake

One Christmas a friend and I baked twenty-four of these cakes, aging them for two weeks before giving them as gifts for the holidays. This recipe makes twelve cakes.

    3-1/2 lb. dried mixed fruit
    3 lb. raisins
    16 cups amazake (p. 161) or hard cider
    8 cups whole wheat pastry flour
    7 cups rye flour
    6 Tbsp. orange or tangerine rind
    12 tsp. cinnamon
    6 tsp. cloves

2-3 tsp. ginger (to taste)
4 cups roasted chopped almonds
2 tsp. sea salt

Soak the dried fruits in amazake or cider to cover overnight. Squeeze out and reserve the excess liquid, and dice fruit into bite-size pieces. Add flours to the liquid and let sit at least a few hours. Combine the fruit and flour mixtures with the rest of the ingredients and beat until batter is smooth and thick enough to drop with difficulty from a wooden spoon.

Oil and flour 12–14 small cake molds. Fill pan two-thirds full, cover and steam 1-1/2 hours in preheated 300°F oven. Remove cover and bake until cake pulls away from the sides of the pan and is firm. Place on cake racks to cool.

*To age:* When the cake has cooled completely, remove from pan; dip a piece of cheesecloth into hard cider or amazake, wrap it around the cake and cover tightly with a dry piece of cheesecloth and brown paper. If you have a tin can (an old coffee can will do nicely), place the wrapped cake in the can and store it for a few weeks in a dry, cool place.

## Coffee Cheesecake

This cake tends to be very light and delicate. It would be best to use a springform pan, so that it does not have to be disturbed after baking.

OAT CRUST:
    1/2 cup whole wheat flour
    1 cup rolled oats
    1/4 cup roasted sesame seeds
    1 Tbsp. instant grain coffee
    2 tsp. cinnamon
    1/4 tsp. sea salt
    1/4 cup oil
    1/4 cup maple syrup

    1/4–1/2 cup apple juice or cider
FILLING:
    4 cups mashed tofu
    2 eggs
    1/2 cup maple syrup
    1 tsp. lemon juice
    1 Tbsp. lemon or orange rind
    1 tsp. vanilla
    1/2 tsp. sea salt
    3 Tbsp. arrowroot flour

*Crust*
Roast flour separately until lightly browned. Roast rolled oats until lightly browned. Combine all dry ingredients. Mix oil and sweetener together and add to dry mixture. Use apple juice if necessary.

Preheat oven to 375°F. Oil an 8-inch springform pan, and press crust in the bottom only. Prebake 12 minutes. Set aside.

*Filling*
Mash tofu. Separate eggs. Combine yolks and sweetener, beating quickly until creamy. Slowly add mashed tofu, beating constantly. Add next three ingredients, and sprinkle in arrowroot flour, mixing until arrowroot is no longer visible. For best result use a blender or electric mixer.

Beat egg whites with pinch of salt until peaked. Fold into first mixture carefully. *Do not beat.*

Spoon into prebaked crust, and bake in a preheated 350°F oven 30–40 minutes or until center is almost firm when pan is shaken.

When baked, turn off the oven and let cake sit an additional 30 minutes with the oven door slightly ajar. Remove from the oven and set on a rack to cool.

Remove from pan. Just before serving, top with any glaze.

## Daniel's Strawberry Cheesecake

FILLING:
    1 cup Fruit Purée (p. 64)

4 Tbsp. tahini
1 Tbsp. vanilla
1/2 tsp. sea salt
10 cups hot tofu
CORN CRUST:
    1 cup whole wheat pastry flour
    1 cup corn flour
    5 Tbsp. oil
    3 Tbsp. concentrated sweetener
    1/2 cup apple juice or water
    Strawberry Glaze
TOPPING:
    2 Tbsp. arrowroot flour
    1-1/2 cups apple juice or cider
    1/4 cup concentrated sweetener
      (optional)
    1/4 tsp. sea salt
    4 cups chopped strawberries

*Filling*

Combine purée, tahini, vanilla and sea salt. Blend until creamy. Add tofu and continue to blend 3–5 minutes longer. (If there is not enough liquid, add enough to form a creamy consistency.) Set aside.

*Corn crust*

Roast the flours separately until they begin to brown lightly. Set aside to cool.

Combine flours and salt together in a mixing bowl. Cut the oil into the flour. Add sweetener and enough liquid to form a semimoist crust. Preheat oven to 350°F and oil an 8-inch springform pan. Press crust into the bottom of the pan. Sprinkle extra crust in another pan, and bake both 10 minutes. Set extra crust aside for the sides of the cake. Pour tofu mixture into the bottom of the crust. Bake 25–30 minutes or until the pie is almost solid (shake pan). Remove from oven and place on a rack to cool. When completely cool, remove sides of pan. Press baked crust into the sides of the cake. Cool at room temperature 3 to 6 hours longer.

*Topping*

Dissolve the arrowroot flour in juice or cider. Add sweetener if used, and decrease liquid content accordingly. Cook on a medium heat, stirring constantly until mixture boils; add sea salt and strawberries. Stir rapidly until mixture boils again. Spoon over cake.

## Melon Cheesecake

Follow the recipe for Coffee Cheesecake. While prebaking crust, mix together 1 Tbsp. arrowroot, juice of 1/2 lemon, 1/4 cup sweetener and 1 cup crushed cantaloupe. Place in a pan and cook over a low heat until the mixture boils, thickens and turns clearer. Cool slightly and pour into a prebaked crust. Allow to set.

Pour tofu-cheese mixture over melon mixture. Sprinkle top with crushed nuts.

Bake at 350°F for 40–50 minutes. Turn off heat and let stand in the oven, with the oven door slightly ajar, until cool. Place on rack, remove from pan and serve.

**Cantaloupe Melon (*Cucumis melo*)**
Many kinds of melon exist today. The flesh of a melon consists of about 90 to 95 percent water and only about 5 percent sugar. Melon plants have hairy stems, bearing many leaves which are quite large in size. An annual trailing plant, which probably originated in the tropics, it has given rise to many forms, and many cultivated varieties have been developed, varying in size, shape, color and taste. Cantaloupe melons have deep grooves on the outside running vertically around the whole melon. Mainly used as the first or last course in a meal, they can be incorporated into many different desserts.

## Date Cream Cake

CRUST:
>3/4 cup corn or maize meal
>2 cups whole wheat flour
>1/3 cup oil
>1/4 cup crushed nuts
>1/2 tsp. sea salt
>Apple juice or cider

CAKE MIXTURE I:
>8 cups tofu
>1/2 cup tahini
>2 tsp. vanilla
>1/4 tsp. sea salt
>1/4 cup oil
>1 cup date purée (p. 64)

CAKE MIXTURE II:
>2 cups date purée
>3/4 cup arrowroot flour
>1/4 tsp. sea salt
>2 tsp. orange rind

ICING:
>Instant Tofu Cream (p. 147)
>Coconut (optional)

*Crust*

Roast maize meal until lightly browned. Separately dry roast whole wheat flour until lightly browned. Combine flours, nuts and sea salt. Add apple juice or cider until the dough begins to stick together. Preheat oven at 375°F and oil an 8-inch springform pan. Press the crust mixture into the bottom of pan and prebake 10 minutes.

*Cake mixture I*

Blend tofu, tahini, vanilla, salt, oil, and date purée until creamy. Set aside.

*Cake mixture II*

Combine 2 cups date purée with the arrowroot flour, 1/4 tsp. salt and orange rind. Mix until smooth.

*Putting it all together*

Remove crust from oven and pour the first mixture into it. Swirl the second mixture into the first, until the batter is marbled.

Lower oven temperature to 350°F and bake 25–30 minutes. Remove cake from oven and place on a rack to cool. When cake has cooled completely, remove the sides of the pan. Leave outside until cold. (The longer the cake is aged, the better it will taste.)

Prepare icing before serving and decorate, trim, or sprinkle with coconut.

## Fruit Cake I

>1/2 cup dried fruit
>1/2 cup raisins or sultanas
>1 cup hard cider or stout
>1 tsp. orange, tangerine or lemon rind
>1 tsp. vanilla
>1/4 cup oil
>1/4 cup concentrated sweetener
>1/4 tsp. sea salt
>1 cup whole wheat pastry flour
>3 eggs
>1 cup almond paste

ALMOND PASTE:
>1 lb. almonds
>2 egg whites or apple juice
>1 cup concentrated sweetener

Preheat oven to 350°F. Oil and lightly flour the bottom of an 8-inch round pan (preferably springform).

Soak dried fruit and raisins in hard cider to cover until soft. Squeeze out excess liquid. Dice fruit. Combine fruits and rind in a bowl. Add vanilla, oil and sweetener. Let stand at least 30 minutes. Combine sea salt and flour. Add the fruit to the flour mixture. Set aside. Beat the eggs until double in volume, then fold into fruit mixture until the eggs are no longer visible.

Pour half of batter into cake pan. Cover with Almond Paste. Add remaining batter and bake 60–70 minutes or until cake is springly to the touch and pulls away from the sides of the pan. Remove from the oven and cool on a cake rack.

*Almond paste*

Blanch almonds (p. 16) and pound with

a mortor and pestle or blend adding a little hot apple juice, or egg whites.

When well pounded, place the mixture in a pan, add sweetener and cook, stirring constantly until the mixture thickens.

## Fruit Cake II

Follow the recipe for Fruit Cake I, omitting eggs. Add 1 cup more flour and enough cider to form a pancake-like batter. Steam covered for the first 45 minutes, remove cover and bake 20–30 minutes longer.

## Light Lemon Cake

1-1/2 Tbsp. dry yeast
4 cups apple juice or cider
1/2 cup concentrated sweetener
3 cups sifted whole wheat pastry flour
1 cup arrowroot flour
1/4 cup oil
2 blended lemons
1 tsp. vanilla
1/4 tsp. sea salt

Dilute yeast in 1 cup warm apple juice or cider and let sit until bubbly.

Add enough pastry flour to form a thin batter. Cover and let rise in a warm place until it doubles in size.

Add the rest of the ingredients and beat well. It should resemble a thick pancake batter in consistency, thick enough to drop from a wooden spoon with difficulty (adjust flour-liquid content accordingly).

Preheat the oven to 350°F and oil a small round or square cake pan. Place batter in pan, cover and let rise in a warm place until batter almost reaches the top of the pan.

Bake about 30–40 minutes, or until cake is springly to the touch and pulls away from the side of the pan. Remove from oven and place on a rack to cool.

## Apple-almond Topping

2 Tbsp. oil
2 apples, sliced and cored (peel if not organic)
1/2 cup roasted chopped almonds or walnuts
1/2 cup raisins or currants
1/2 tsp. cinnamon
1/4 tsp. sea salt

Heat oil in a skillet. When oil is hot, sauté apples lightly. Add nuts, raisins or currants, cinnamon and salt. Cook on a low flame for 5 minutes. Spoon over cake.

## Upside-down Peach Cake

2 Tbsp. oil
1/4 cup concentrated sweetener
4 peaches
2 eggs
2–3 cups boiling apple juice or cider
2 cups sifted whole wheat pastry flour
1 Tbsp. cinnamon
1 tsp. sea salt
1/2 cup chopped roasted nuts
2 Tbsp. orange rind
1 tsp. vanilla

Preheat the oven to 350°F. Oil and lightly flour the bottom of a 6×8-inch pan. Heat oil and sweetener together. Core and slice peaches (peel if not organic). Mix peaches into the oil-sweetener combination. Set aside.

Beat eggs, gradually adding juice or cider, and vanilla. Add sifted flour, cinnamon and sea salt to the egg mixture. Mix in nuts and rind.

Place peach mixture decoratively into the pan, pour batter over the peaches and bake 20–30 minutes, or until set. Remove from oven and place on a rack to cool. Turn upside-down, remove pan and serve.

**Variations**

1. Add 2 Tbsp. orange rind to egg mixture before adding boiling juice.
2. Substitute berries for peaches.
3. Soak 1 cup dried fruit in liquid to cover until soft. Squeeze out excess liquid; dice and substitute for peaches.
4. Add 1/4 tsp. cloves, 1/2 tsp. ginger and 1 tsp. lemon, orange or tangerine rind to flour and sea salt before combining with egg mixture.

## Black and White Birthday Cake

Another excuse to bake a cake: a birthday!

WHITE LAYER:
> 3 eggs
> 1/2 cup oil
> 1 tsp. vanilla
> 1/4 tsp. sea salt
> 1/2 tsp. lemon juice
> 1/4 cup concentrated sweetener
> 1/2 cup sifted whole wheat pastry flour
> Apple juice or cider if necessary

BLACK LAYER:
> 3 eggs
> 1/2 cup oil
> 1 tsp. orange rind
> 1/4 tsp. sea salt
> 1-1/2 cups raisin purée (p. 64)
> 1 cup sifted whole wheat pastry flour

ICING:
> 2 cups Icing (p. 60)

*White layer*

Separate eggs. Combine yolks, oil and vanilla. Stir and set aside. Oil and lightly flour two 7-inch round springform pans. Beat whites gradually, adding sea salt and lemon juice, until they are stiff. Add sweetener slowly, drop by drop, beating continuously until whites are peaked. Fold a quarter of the whites into the yolks. Pour this mixture over the remaining whites. Fold in the sifted flour gently until the whites are no longer visible. *Do not over-mix.*

Preheat the oven to 350°F.

Pour into pan. Do not pat down. Bake 30–40 minutes at 350°F, or until cake is puffy and pulls away from the sides of the pan. Turn off oven, leave door slightly ajar until cake is cool.

*Black layer*

Follow the directions for white layer, substituting in appropriate places.

*Putting it all together*

When both layers have cooled, place the black layer top side down, and spread icing over it. Place the white layer on top and ice the sides of the cake (p. 54). You may wish to roll the sides in crushed nuts, rind, etc. Cover top with icing and decorate as desired. Refer to chapter 3—for other decorating ideas.

**Variation**

Substitute 1 cup arrowroot for whole wheat pastry flour, in black layer. Bake at 350°F 10–12 minutes or until *almost* solid. *Overbaking* may make the cake rubbery.

## Pumpkin Cake

> 1/2 cup concentrated sweetener
> 6 egg yolks
> 1/2 cup unrefined corn oil
> 1 cup pumpkin purée (p. 63)
> 2 cups sifted whole wheat pastry flour
> 2 tsp. cinnamon
> 3/4 tsp. cloves
> 1/2 tsp. nutmeg
> 1/2 cup crushed roasted sunflower seeds
> 1 Tbsp. orange rind
> 6 egg whites
> Pinch of sea salt
> 1 Tbsp. orange juice

Beat sweetener and yolks together until the mixture looks like thick cream. Slowly drip in the oil and continue beating until fully absorbed. Mix in pumpkin.

Sift together next four ingredients. Add sunflower seeds and rind, and fold into first mixture.

Beat egg whites with a pinch of sea salt and orange juice until stiff peaks form. Gently fold about 1/3 of the egg whites into the batter, then add remaining whites to batter, folding gently. Preheat oven to 350°F.

Bake in oiled and floured cake tins about 50–60 minutes or until cake tests done. Turn off oven and leave door slightly ajar. Leave cake there until cool. Remove from pan, and when completely cool, ice if desired.

## Corn Cake

> 1/2 cup raisins
> Apple juice, cider, mu tea or mint tea to cover raisins
> 1/2 cup sifted chestnut flour
> 2 eggs
> 1/2 cup oil
> Corn from 3 ears, grated
> 1/2 tsp. sea salt
> 1/2 cup sifted whole wheat pastry flour

Soak raisins in juice or tea until soft. Roast chestnut flour until lightly browned. Set aside to cool.

Separate eggs; combine yolks, oil, corn and 1/4 tsp. sea salt. Mix well.

Sift pastry flour and chestnut flour into mixing bowl. Add yolk mixture and stir, then add raisins and mix well until all ingredients are thoroughly combined.

Beat whites, adding remaining sea salt gradually, until they form stiff peaks. Preheat oven to 375°F. Fold one quarter of the flour mixture into whites. Pour egg-white mixture over remaining batter,' and *fold* in gently until white disappears. *Do not overmix.* Consistency should be that of a fluffy pancake-like batter.

Place batter in oiled round or square 6-inch cake pan. *Do not pat down.* Bake 40–45 minutes, or until lightly browned and puffy. Turn off oven and open door slightly, leave cake there until cool.

## Swiss Roll

SPONGE:
> 3 yolks
> 1/4 cup concentrated sweetener
> 3 egg whites
> 1/4 tsp. sea salt
> 1 tsp. vanilla
> 1 Tbsp. orange rind
> 1 cup sifted whole wheat pastry flour

FILLING:
> 1 Chestnut Cream (p. 144)
> Carob Frosting (p. 61)

Preheat oven to 375°F and line the bottom of an 8 × 11 × 1/2-inch baking sheet with grease-proof paper. Oil well.

Beat yolks and sweetener together until creamy and light. Set aside.

Beat whites and salt together until stiff peaks form. Beat in vanilla and rind.

Sift whole wheat flour into yolk mixture and fold in gently.

Fold 1/3 of the egg whites into yolk mixture, then fold the rest of the egg whites in *very gently.*

Spoon into baking pan, bake 12–15 minutes or until sponge is lightly browned and pulls away from the sides of the pan.

Immediately remove sponge from pan, and place on a towel or cloth.

Peel off the paper, trim the edges so that it will roll without splitting. Spread with filling. Roll up sheet tightly in the towel or cloth. Let stand on a rack to cool.

Glaze before serving.

### Variation

After baking sponge, cut into strips and sandwich them together, spreading chestnut cream in between each layer. Spoon Carob Frosting over top.

## Taki's Upside-down Cake

Souen is a small Japanese natural food restaurant, located on Manhattan's upper West Side. Many years ago when Taki decided to open this restaurant, he asked me to be the baker. This was my first venture into the world of professional dessert making and this my first successful creation.

My gratitude to Taki.

    1 Tbsp. dry yeast
    1–2 cups warm apple juice or cider
    2 cups whole wheat pastry flour
    2 Tbsp. oil
    1 tsp. vanilla
    1/2 tsp. sea salt
    1/4 cup concentrated sweetener
APPLE-WALNUT TOPPING:
    2 Tbsp. oil
    2 apples, sliced and cored (peel if not organic)
    1/2 cup roasted chopped walnuts
    1/2 cup raisins or currants
    1 tsp. cinnamon
    1/4 tsp. sea salt

*Topping*
Heat oil in a skillet. When oil is hot, sauté apples lightly. Add nuts, raisins or currants, cinnamon and sea salt. Cook on a low heat for 5 minutes. Set aside.

*Cake*
Combine first two ingredients. Set aside until it bubbles. Mix. Add flour and beat. Cover and set aside to rise.

Preheat oven to 350°F. Oil and lightly flour an 8-inch cake pan or two small ones. After batter has doubled, add the rest of the ingredients, and beat with a wooden spoon about 10 minutes. The consistency should be that of a thick pancake batter (adjust flour-liquid content accordingly).

Place topping in the oiled cake pan. Pour batter over topping until pan is half full. Cover and let rise in a warm place, until almost double in size.

Bake about 30–45 minutes, or until top is slightly browned and springly to the touch. Remove from oven and place on a rack to cool.

## Valentine Cake

    2 cups uncooked couscous
    4 Tbsp. oil
    1 tsp. sea salt
    5 cups boiling apple juice or cider
    1-1/2 bars agar-agar
    1 Tbsp dried mint

Sauté couscous until well coated with oil (2 Tbsp. oil for 1 cup couscous). Place in a mixing bowl and add sea salt and 3 cups juice or cider. Stir well. Set aside. Rinse agar-agar under cold running water quickly. Squeeze out excess liquid. Shred into small pieces and combine with remaining apple juice or cider. Bring to a boil, lower heat and cook together with mint until agar-agar dissolves. Add couscous to agar-agar mixture and stir until well combined.

Rinse a heart-shaped mold under cold running water; dry well and oil. Place couscous into mold *immediately* after cooking (if too much time elapses, the mixture will begin to set). Cool. Turn out cake on platter.

## Almond Topping

> 1 cup almond butter
> 1/4 cup concentrated sweetener
> 1 tsp. vanilla
> 1 tsp. lemon rind
> 1/4 cup ground roasted almonds
> 1/2–1 cup apple juice or cider

Combine almond butter with sweetener, mixing until a thick paste is formed. Add vanilla, lemon rind and almonds. Mix well. You may find that this mixture is too thick for a blender because the thickness of almond butter varies, depending on the oil content. It may sometimes be necessary to add some apple juice to thin.

### Variation
Substitute 1 cup tahini or any nut butter for almond butter.

## Festive Cakes

The most celebrated festival of the ancients occurred at the time of the year when the sun was beginning to regain its power. Called "Yule," it was a time of mingling, feasting, drinking and dancing, with sacrifices and religious rites for all. Presents were exchanged between masters and slaves, family and friends, all of whom were then considered to be on an equal basis.

At such time of thanksgiving and rejoicing, the kitchen becomes the center of all joy, radiating with restless anticipation as imaginative cooks create festive delicacies. The following recipes are offered to assist you on your way to creating glowing faces, starry songs, bright eyes and happy smiles for all special occasions.

## Christmas Tree Cake

Use this cake as the base for any special occasion cake, choosing fillings and icings to complement the theme. See Chapter 3 for decorating ideas.

> 5 cups raisins
> 2 tsp. vanilla
> 2 tsp. cinnamon
> 1/2 tsp. cloves
> 1 Tbsp. orange or lemon rind
> 1/2 tsp. salt
> 1/4 cup oil
> 1–2 cups apple juice
> 1-1/2 Tbsp. dry yeast
> 3 cups sifted whole wheat pastry flour

Combine raisins, vanilla, spices, salt, rind and oil in a large mixing bowl. Add enough juice to cover. Set aside the night before or several hours before using.

Oil cake tin. Flour the bottom of forms lightly.

In a separate bowl, dissolve yeast in 4 Tbsp. warm juice. Set aside until it bubbles. Add enough flour to yeast mixture to form a thin batter. Beat for a few minutes. Cover and let rise in a warm place until batter doubles in size.

Blend the raisin mixture until smooth and creamy. When the batter has risen, beat it down with a wooden spoon and combine it with the raisin mixture. Stir for a few minutes until well combined. Add the rest of the flour and salt to the raisin-yeast mixture. Consistency should be that of a thick pancake batter, dropping from a wooden spoon with difficulty (adjust flour-liquid content accordingly).

Fill the form 1/2–2/3 full. Cover with the same size form and let rise in a warm place until batter reaches top of form. Preheat the oven to 350°F. Bake 30–45 minutes, or until the cake is springly to the touch and pulls away from the sides of the pan.

## Variations
1. Add 1–2 cups dried chopped fruit (soak before adding) after blending in raisin mixture.
2. Add 1 cup chopped roasted nuts or seeds to batter after combining the two mixtures (toss lightly with flour before adding).
3. Add 1 tsp. dried ginger, or 4–6 tsp. grain coffee to raisin mixture before soaking.

TOPPING:
    2–3 cups Instant Tofu Cream (p. 147)
    2–3 tsp. beet juice
DECORATIONS:
    Orange rind
    Mint (dried)
    Almonds
    Raisins
    Sesame seeds

*Making a Christmas Tree Cake*
1. Cut a 1-inch strip from bottom of cake.
2. Cut cake diagonally.
3. Arrange (see illustration).
4. Mark sloping sides into four or five equal parts, and at each mark cut in about 1 inch.
5. Cut out diagonally to meet first cut. Set aside small cut-out triangles to use for Petit Fours (p. 38).
6. Cut 1-inch strip into three. Arrange to

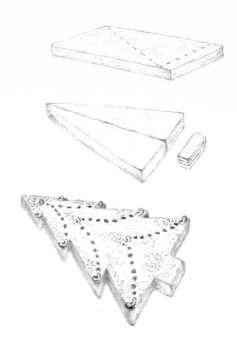

form trunk of tree. Spread a small amount of Tofu Cream in between slices to hold them together.
7. Spread a small amount of Tofu Cream in between two triangles, and put them together to form tree.
8. Attach trunk to tree and ice.

*Topping*
Prepare Instant Tofu Cream, adding beet juice to half of the Tofu Cream for coloring. Add mint to the other half. Trim the edges of the cake on all four sides before frosting.

*Decorating*
Spread the Tofu Cream over the entire tree, alternating the colors.

Place nuts on the tips of the branches, sprinkling orange rind and mint on the edges and the top. Place raisins and nuts on the edges.

## Holiday Feast

    1 recipe Christmas Tree Cake (p. 47)
APPLE CUSTARD FILLING
    3 apples

Juice and rind of 1/2 lemon
2 Tbsp. concentrated sweetener
1 Tbsp. roasted whole wheat pastry flour
1/2 tsp. sea salt
1/4–1/2 cup apple juice or cider
2 egg yolks (room temperature)
1 tsp. vanilla
1 tsp. cinnamon
2 Tbsp. oil
COFFEE TOPPING
4 Tbsp. oil
2 Tbsp. concentrated sweetener
2 Tbsp. grain coffee substitute
1 tsp. vanilla
1/2 tsp. sea salt
1 egg
2 cups cookie, cake or bread crumbs
2 Tbsp. shredded, unsweetened coconut

*Apple custard filling*

Grate apples (peel if not organic). Combine apples, lemon juice and sweetener together. Cook on a medium heat until mixture boils. Add rind.

In a separate pan, dissolve roasted flour and salt in apple juice. Combine with apple mixture, stirring constantly until thickened.

Separate eggs. Stir 2–3 Tbsp. of cooked filling into egg yolks. Put this mixture back in filling, stirring rapidly. Return to heat and cook in a double boiler on a low heat, stirring constantly until mixture thickens. Remove from heat, stir in vanilla, spice and oil. Chill before using.

*Coffee topping*

Combine oil, sweetener, grain coffee substitute, vanilla and sea salt in the top of a double boiler. Cook over simmering water a few minutes. Stir in lightly beaten egg. Continue cooking, stirring constantly until mixture begins to thicken. Add crumbs and coconut. Refrigerate when cool.

*Putting it all together*

Cut each layer of the cake horizontally in half. Place layer on rack and put cookie sheet under rack to catch drippings. Drip hard cider evenly over the layers.

Place one layer on a plate, top side down, putting strips of wax paper on all four corners of the plate before setting down the layer. This enables you to decorate the cake on the same plate that you serve it on.

Spread layer with custard filling. Repeat layering and filling, placing each layer top side down, ending with cake layer.

*Topping*

Frost sides and top of cake with topping. Decorate cake with crushed nuts, orange or tangerine rind. See Chapter 3 "Inside and Outside," for more decorating ideas.

## Lotus Flower Wedding Cake

John and Diana asked me to prepare their wedding cake. Baking this cake for my dearest friends was one of my greatest pleasures.

2 recipes Christmas Tree Cake (p. 47)
Wedding Threads (p. 60)
1 recipe Oat Cream (p. 145)
4 lemons
1/2 cup concentrated sweetener
1/4 tsp. salt
Crushed almonds

Preheat the oven to 350°F. Oil and lightly flour four round cake pans, approximately 8, 7, 6 and 5-inch-size. The layers may be baked in the same-size pans and trimmed down to size after baking. Spoon batter into pans and bake 30–45 minutes or until cake pulls away from the sides of the pan and is springy to the touch.

This cake may be baked one day in advance and stored tightly sealed in a cool place until ready to use.

*Decorations*

Prepare Oat Cream, adding lemon rind to taste after cooking.

Cut the peel of 2 lemons into long, thin vertical strips, 1/8 inch thick. Combine concentrated sweetener and lemon peel in a pot and bring to a boil.

Lower heat, and boil down until dry and candied.

Grate the rind of the other 2 lemons. Set aside.

*Putting it all together*

Trim the sides of the layers and prepare the cake for decorating (p. 53). Place the layers on top of each other to make sure that they decrease in size proportionately. Spread Oat Cream between the layers and place them upside-down on top of each other. If the layers are too thick, cut them in half horizontally and spread Oat Cream between the cut layers first. Prepare Wedding Threads.

Peak Icing over the entire cake.

*Flower Shaping*

Draw a petal, 1 inch smaller than half the width of the top layer, on a heavy piece of paper. Cut it out, and place it on top of the cake, marking the design on the icing in the shape of a 6 or 8-petal lotus. Remove the pattern and place the candied lemon peel on the lines forming the lotus. Sprinkle the grated lemon rind inside the petals.

*Finishing Touches*

Sprinkle almonds around the edges of the cake.

## Sweet Aveline

It was just the beginning of Pisces, and Aveline Kushi's birthday. I was asked to bake a birthday cake and chose to decorate it with the symbol of Pisces—two fish.

3 recipes (10 cups) Chestnut Cream
(p. 144)

2 Basic Cakes (p. 37)
2 cups Icing (p. 60)
INLAY:
Outline of fish—pine nuts
Scales—small pieces of orange skin and rind
Tail—thin strips of lemon skin
Mouth—thin strips of lemon skin
Eye—raisin
String attaching two fish—mint or sesame seeds

Bake cake several hours (or even 24 hours) in advance. Wrap well in foil to keep fresh.

Prepare Chestnut Cream.

Prepare Icing.

Oil an 11 × 16-inch baking sheet very well. Make the outline of the design using the ingredients listed above.

Spoon Chestnut Cream very carefully over the design covering the entire surface of the pan. Allow to set.

Remove Basic Cake from pan. Trim off edges. Spread Icing on top.

To unmold cream place Basic Cake on top of cream. Hold it fast and flip them both over at the same time.

Allow the mold to fall naturally.

Remove baking pan.

Insert strips of wax paper underneath cake (see Pre-decorating Techniques, p. 53). Ice and decorate. Chill before serving.

# 3. INSIDE AND OUTSIDE: *Icings, Glazes, Purées, Fillings, Toppings*

Enjoyment can be derived from making cakes, pies, pastries, or whatever you have prepared, pleasing to the eye as well as to the palate. Here are some ideas to help you think about making desserts just as attractive on the outside as they are delicious on the inside.

## General Equipment for Decorating

Pastry bags
Metal tubes in various sizes to use for piping or fluting (see p. 57)
Cake racks or drying racks

Extra cake pans or cardboard forms the same size or slightly larger than the cake being decorated
Metal and rubber spatulas

Pastry brushes
Blender
Wire whisk
Food mill
Double boiler

Electric mixer or rotary hand beater
Brown wax or greaseproof paper
Cookie or baking sheet (to catch drippings when decorating)
Cake-decorating stand (optional)

# Choosing the Decoration or Filling

There are many different kinds of decorations and fillings to choose from; each with a special look and texture of its own. Choose one or more according to the type of cake or pastry, the look, shape, taste and texture you want it to have, and where and when you want to serve it.

### Butter Icings and Fillings

Made from a nut-butter base, and embellished with fruit and spices, this type of decoration can give a creamy effect as well as a stiff peaked look. Try it for fillings or icings, fluting or piping, using a pastry bag for added effect.

### Creams (see p. 144)

*Egg-based.* Made with the yolk, white, or whole egg, these are desirable for fillings as well as toppings.
*Flour-based.* Usually made from pastry, corn or chestnut flour, they too are perfect for filling pies or pastries.
*Grain-based.* Made from rolled, steel-cut or whole oats, barley or rice. Cooked, blended and flavored, they form a delicious creamy base filling or topping on the inside and outside of any kind of dessert.

*Tofu.* This cream can be used for any purpose, such as icings, toppings and fillings, or as a separate cold dessert.

### Glazes

Gives a smooth, shiny appearance for any kind of cake, pie or pastry.

### Fruit or Vegetable Purée

Simple, but tasty, these blends of fruits and/or vegetables and added flavoring, such as rinds or vanilla, can embellish any pastry or cake. Use as a filling, topping or trim.

### Concentrated Sweetener (see p. 163)

Fruit concentrates, maple syrup, grain honey, molasses, barley malt, maltose, apple butter, apple cider jelly, amazake, grain syrup, fruit purée.

### Syrups

Heated and used alone or cooked with kuzu or arrowroot and flavored with nuts, rind, spices or fruit, this form of topping can present a glowing appearance, as well as a delicious taste.

# Pre-decorating Techniques

1. Cool the cake completely.
2. Trim off the hard, crisp edges (about 1/8 inch) from the side.
3. Check to see if layers are level. If not, cut away some of top of cake, so that they are level when sandwiched together. If top layer is too irregular, level off top and invert.
4. Brush away all loose crumbs.
5. Place cake (or layer) upside-down on platter.
6. Cut four strips of wax paper at least 4 inches wide and long enough to cover surface of the platter that the cake is being served on.
7. Lifting the cake with a spatula, place the strips of wax paper 2 inches underneath the bottom, extending them a few inches outward.
8. After decorating the cake, allow icing to dry before removing wax paper.

# Finishing Touches

## Before Baking

Brush or spread any glaze (p. 61) on top of yeasted and unyeasted pastries, covered pies, tarts and rolled cookies.

## During Baking

Brush the tops with oil, or concentrated sweetener, or any glaze, 10 minutes before removing from oven.

### Decorations baked on the cake
Some decorations can be put onto a cake before it is baked.

*Nuts:* Unroasted nuts are usually easy to apply before baking and look attractive on top of a cake. For very special occasions, blanch the nuts before scattering them on top of the cake (see p. 16).

To make a glaze over nuts, you may brush a little egg white carefully over the unroasted or blanched nuts before baking.

*Rind:* Plain cakes look more attractive if you sprinkle orange or lemon rind on top. If baking period is long, sprinkle the rind gently on top of the cake three quarters of the way through the baking time.

*Crumb topping:* If the cake has a long baking period, sprinkle the crumb topping (p. 66) on halfway through the baking time allotted.

*Pastry as a decoration:* Pastry can be used as a decoration, especially if you are making pastry and batter cakes on the same day. Use a lattice design of pasty over a fruit cake or any design you choose on top of any cake. Be sure that proper time is alloted to bake the pastry as well as the cake.

## After Baking

Brush the tops of yeasted or unyeasted pastries, covered pies, tarts, cookies and petit fours with concentrated sweetener *before* the dessert cools, preferably immediately after baking. Do not pour hot glaze over warm cakes or petit fours; allow these to cool completely before glazing. Spoon glaze on cakes after cooling, sprinkle roasted nuts, seeds or crumb topping on top of glaze. (Or, the nuts, seeds etc., may be placed on the dessert before glazing, and the glaze spooned or brushed carefully over them.)

To prepare cakes and petit fours for glazing, follow these steps before proceeding:
(1) Trim off hard, crisp edges. (2) Place cake on a rack. (3) Place a pan or cookie sheet under the rack to catch the drippings. (4) Spoon hot glaze over the top of the cake, allowing it to drip down the sides. (5) Coat sides before or after glazing. (It is good to spread a base of butter icing, cream or glaze over the cakes before putting on the final icing.)

Choose one of the following:
1.  Spread the icing over the top of the cake. Draw a small knife across the icing to give a ridged effect.

2.  Spread icing over top and sides of a cake. Mark the top with a fork, by moving it across the icing in a wavy line. Coat sides with roasted nuts or seeds, etc.
3.  Spread a nut butter icing over the top of a cake rather thickly. (Use a cold icing that has been chilled.) Sweep the point of a knife or the prongs of a fork or the back of a spoon over the icing, and at the same time, lift it in peaks. Do not try to do this evenly, since it looks more effective if it is slightly uneven.

4.  Place a doily on top of the cake. Shake or sprinkle roasted chestnut flour, orange or lemon rind, or crushed roasted nuts or seeds on top of the doily. Lift the doily carefully, with one upward sweep.
5.  To glaze or ice only the top of the cake, tie or pin a strong band of paper around the sides of the cake. Put any agar-agar topping on top of the cake. Allow to set before removing paper.
6.  Prepare an icing or glaze that is stiffer, by using less liquid. Spread over top and sides of cake. When top starts to harden, take the edge of a knife and go around the rim of the cake, sweeping upward.
7.  A broken line effect can be gotten by spreading the butter icing roughly over the cake. It usually forms a rough-looking texture. If you want to follow a definite design, push it very gently with a knife.
8.  Lattice design can be produced by using butter icing and different colored jellies or fruit butters. Mark the lattice design on the top of the cake that has been given a thin layer of icing on top. Pipe either straight or slightly wavy lines following the marks. Fill the centers between lines with jelley or fruit butter. (The jelly or fruit butter can also be applied to the top of the cake using a pastry bag.) If the jelly or butter is too stiff, mix with a small quantity of warm liquid.
9.  Smooth-looking nut butter icing can be made by using a knife that is long enough to cover the entire width of the cake, holding it at both ends at an angle and pulling it toward you.
10.  Swirl the nut butter icing using a knife and a sharp upward motion after each swirl.
11.  To obtain a line effect with nut butter icing, use a tea knife or very thin palette knife. Make a sweep from the center of the cake to the edge and then follow this line all around. This is difficult to do around the

sides of the cake, so straight or wavy lines are better there.

Hold a spatula, tea knife or very thin palette knife at the center of the cake. Turn the cake slowly, and move the spatula gradually to the outer edge of the cake or sweep the knife or spatula from the center of the cake to the edge in a semi-circular motion. (Use a nut butter icing for best results.)

12. *Peak:* Using a nut butter icing or Wedding Threads (p. 60), ice the entire cake. Place a spatula on the cake and pull it away to make a series of peaks.

13. *Zigzag:* Cut saw like teeth along the edge of a cardboard slightly larger than the width of the cake, move the cardboard along the top of the cake from side to side.

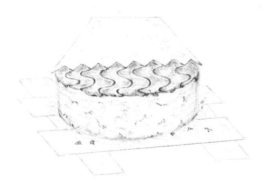

14. *Spiral:* First cover the cake with a dark or light colored icing, then fit a pastry bag with a small round tube and fill the pastry bag with a contrasting colored icing.

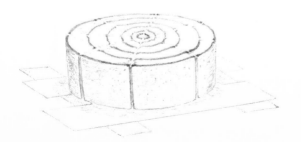

Pipe a series of circles, working from the outer edge of the cake to the center. Draw a thin knife or skewer lightly over the cake, as if cutting a pie into 8 or 12 pieces.

15. *Stencil:* First ice the cake with a stiff nut butter icing. Allow the icing to dry. Cut any pattern or shape out of cardboard and place it on top of the cake. Spread icing or sprinkle roasted chestnut flour, rind, mint or cinnamon over the top of the cardboard where the pattern has been cut out. (Use a contrasting color for best results.)

16. *Feather icing:* Use any light colored icing (tofu cream, oat, barley or rice creams) or light icing tinted with vegetable coloring (p. 18) and any dark icing (nut butter base is best for piping). Place the dark icing in a decorating bag. (Use a plain round tube for the pastry bag. See p. 57.) Spread light or tinted icing on cookie or cover cake with icing. Immediately pipe onto this straight lines, circles, spirals, etc., in dark icing. Use a skewer or toothpick to create design, drawing skewer either in straight lines, circles or swirls.

## Flowers

Choose fresh flowers that do not have poisonous properties and place them on the cake just before serving. Open-petaled flowers that have bright gay colors, arranged delicately, give an attractive finish to any cake.

*Added touch*

For an added touch, use either lemon skin or orange skin, cut into different shapes (thin, long strips, curves) and boil in apple juice until soft. Drain immediately and keep in a bowl of cold water with a pinch of sea salt until using.

Lay flower down. Place strips or curves around the outside of the flower.

Decorating may be used on many different

kinds of food such as cupcakes, petit fours, French pastries, molded agar-agar desserts, salads, cookies and pies. The same method is applied; the only change may be the icing you choose to decorate with.

## Cupcakes

Here are a few ideas for cupcake decorations. An open-star tube was used for most of these designs.

This is another way of decorating a cupcake:

Cut off the top third of the cupcake. Cut this piece in half down the center.

Ice the bottom of the cupcake with a heavy nut butter icing or Wedding Threads (p. 60).

Place the two halves of the top section at an angle in an upright position on top of the cupcake. Decorate with the rest of the icing, nuts and dried fruit.

## Nuts as Decorations

Nuts can add an attractive appearance to any cake, pie or pastry, as well as an enjoyable taste and texture.

*Blanched:* Blanched nuts add a certain finished look to a cake. They may be used after icing or before baking. If placing blanched nuts on top of a cake after baking, use some concentrated sweetener, nut butter icing, or cream to make them adhere properly.

*Whole, halves or split:* Good to use for border decoration. Place them around the top edge of a cake before or after baking.

*Chopped, shredded or slivered:* Sprinkle them over cakes, pies or roll sides of iced cake before decorating top.

## Necessary Items

Cake decorating is fascinating and simple to do. It is something everyone can learn, but it requires perseverance, patience and practice. Once you acquire the knack of working with a pastry bag, you will be able to serve attractive and skillfully decorated pastries, cakes, cookies and pies, which will elicit compliments not only for taste, but for looks as well.

I began to learn cake decorating when two of my friends asked me to make their wedding cake. I bought myself a pastry bag, four basic tubes, and a cake decorating book, and began to practice piping and fluting on upside-down bowls, baking pans, cookie sheets, cardboard boxes, wax paper— anything that could be decorated. In a short time I was able to create homemade cakes that looked as lavishly glamorous as anything I had seen in a bakery store.

My mother used to take a piece of heavy brown paper, roll it into a cone, fill it with icing, snip off the tip and squeeze. Out came "magic" flowers, spirals, borders, even words . . . Today, most stores are supplied with pastry bags and various tubes which offer a great variety of ways to fashion pastries, cakes and pies into tantalizing desserts.

In order to accomplish quick and easy decoration, the following items are necessary:

*One or two 14-inch bags.* These should be large enough to use for creams, cookie batters or fillings, and small enough to handle gracefully.

*A plain round tube.* There are several different sizes that can be advantageous, depending on what you want to do.

*Round tube*
- 1/4-inch opening can be used for the same filling as the smaller tube, shaping small cookies and for lettering or decorating the top of a cake or pie.
- 1/2-inch opening can be used for making cream puffs, eclairs, cookies and for filling tart shells.
- 3/4-inch opening can be used for any of the above if making or filling a large shell, as well as for larger cookies.

*Star tube*
- Opening slightly larger than 1/4-inch can be used for fillings, and borders on small cakes.
- 1/2-inch openings can be used for cake decorations, kisses, borders and fillings, as well as for shaping small molded cookies.
- 3/4-inch opening can be used for making cookies that contain seeds, dried fruit pieces, or nuts for cake borders or for filling large pie shells or pies.

*Ribbon tube.* This can be used for making cookies as well as for cake decorating. This is a flat tube with one serrated edge having an opening about 3/4-inch long. Press out dough into one long ribbon, and break into 2 to 3-inch lengths before baking.

*Coupling.* With this attachment, you can interchange decorating tubes without having to empty the bag. It also prevents filling from squirting out the side of the bag.

*Revolving cake-decorating stand.* You will find this to be a very useful tool when decorating and icing cakes. It allows you to remain stationary as you decorate, giving you more flexibility in your designs.

## Pastry Bag: Filling and Decorating

*Filling the pastry bag*
1. Insert the coupling into the pastry bag, fitting it into the small end of the tube.
2. Place the tube over the coupling.
3. Screw the coupling nut onto the coupling.
4. Hold the bag in one hand, and, keeping it open, fold the edge over the hand.

*Alternate method for filling*
1. Fit the pastry bag into a large jar, folding the edge over the lip of the jar.
2. Using a rubber spatula, spoon the filling into the pastry bag. Remove excess filling from the spatula by pinching the bag as you withdraw the spatula.
3. Fold over the top or flap of the bag, squeeze down filling, then fold the sides of the bag near the top and twist until a little filling is forced through the tube. *Never put too much filling into the bag.* Leave enough room so that the top may be folded down securely to prevent any filling from oozing out at the top.

*Decorating with Pastry Bag*

With your dominant hand, press down on the top of the twisted bag and squeeze out the filling. Use the other hand to guide the end of the bag. *Do not press the lower end of the bag.* Retwist the top as the bag empties.

*Alternate Method*

Press down on the top of the twisted bag to squeeze out filling. Use the other hand to guide the dominant hand.

*Cookies:* For shaping round cookies, hold the pastry bag vertically above the cookie sheet with the tip about 1/4-inch away from the sheet. Without moving the bag, squeeze out the filling into a 1 or 2-inch round. Pull the bag away quickly. Try other shapes and sizes when you feel comfortable working with the bag.

*Cream puffs:* For shaping cream puffs, hold the bag vertically above the baking sheet with the tip about 3/4 inch away from the sheet. Squeeze out batter, raising the bag slightly, to form a high mound about 2 inches in diameter.

*Borders:* For making fancy borders on cakes, use a star tube with a 3/4-inch opening. Hold the pastry bag at an angle about 1/8 inch away from the cake. Squeeze out the filling by moving the bag back and forth, so that each layer of icing partly covers the previous one. Or, holding the bag vertically, squeeze out filling quickly, finishing each movement by abruptly drawing the bag away straight up. The more you squeeze, the bigger the star.

Drop tubes into a glass of water after using, so the icing does not harden in the tubes.

Practice using a pastry bag, filled with an inexpensive ingredient (eg. potatoes) on sheets of wax paper, upside-down bowls, pans and cardboard boxes.

# Forget Me Knots

1. The amount of liquid necessary for the proper consistency of each recipe will vary according to the moisture and temperature of the flour and the room, the size of the eggs and the general weather of the day. Remain flexible and adjust liquid content accordingly.

2. Mu tea or mint tea may be substituted for liquid in any recipe. If more sweetness is desired, add a few tablespoons of concentrated sweetener (see chart, p. 163), decreasing the liquid content accordingly.

3. When diluting arrowroot in liquid, stir again *immediately before* adding it to the mixture, as arrowroot tends to settle to the bottom rather quickly.

4. Kuzu may be substituted for arrowroot in any recipe.

5. Using agar-agar, arrowroot or kuzu with acid fruits (lemons, tangerines, oranges, strawberries) may cause the mixture to set less firmly. Add 1/4 to 1/2 bar more agar-agar, or 1/2 Tbsp. more arrowroot or kuzu, according to the amount of fruit used and the acidity of the fruit.

6. Double boilers are better to use for heating delicate icing ingredients (especially eggs), which tend to cook rather quickly and burn.

7. Never cook liquid vanilla or citrus rind, as doing so will decrease their flavor.

# Recipes

## Icings

The consistency of nut butter icings can vary, depending upon what you want to do with it. A firm icing is necessary if you want to pipe it onto a cake for decoration. A softer icing is better to use for spreading around the sides of a cake, especially if you want to roll the sides of the cake in nuts, seeds or rind. A delicate, soft, creamy butter icing is nice to make when you are planning to fill or cover the top of a delicate cake. Then, over this delicate thin layer you can pipe fluted edges or write with a firmer nut butter icing.

*Tips*

1. Add a little extra Chestnut Cream (p. 144) or nut butter to make icing stiffer.
2. After adding nut butter or purée, chill several hours before using (icings made with arrowroot flour, however, should be used immediately).
3. To soften icing, add a little warm liquid before using.
4. If icing is too thick, mix with a little concentrated sweetener or juice.
5. Nut butter icing that is going to be used for piping or writing should be made several hours in advance to make it stiffer, so it will maintain its shape after piping. If the icing becomes too stiff and tends to crack, beat in a few drops of hot liquid, or use for marzipan.

## Icing I

> 1 cup tahini, almond or sesame butter
> 1/2 to 1 cup Chestnut Cream (p. 144)
>   to taste
> 2 Tbsp. carob
> 1 tsp. orange or lemon rind
> 1/4 tsp. sea salt

> 1 tsp. vanilla

Blend together tahini, Chestnut Cream and carob.

Add rind, sea salt and vanilla. Keep blending until desired consistency is reached (the longer you blend, the thicker it becomes). Use hot juice to adjust consistency.

## Icing II

> 1 Tbsp. arrowroot flour
> 1 cup apple juice or cider
> 2 Tbsp. any nut butter

Dissolve arrowroot flour in 2 to 3 Tbsp. juice or cider and set aside.

In a heavy saucepan, combine the rest of the juice or nut butter. (For piping, use less juice.) Heat on a medium heat, stirring occasionally. When it is almost boiling, add arrowroot mixture and stir rapidly until mixture comes to a boil, thickens and turns clear. Remove from heat, and ice cake immediately.

## Mocha Butter Icing

Follow the recipe for Icing II. Add 2 Tbsp. grain coffee substitute to juice and nut butter. When mixture is almost boiling, add arrowroot mixture and cook another 2 minutes, stirring rapidly. Remove from heat and stir in 1/2 tsp. cinnamon and 1 tsp. lemon juice.

## Wedding Threads

If you ever have an occasion to decorate a wedding cake, here is an icing that will have everyone's attention before it is eaten and will be long remembered after. It is one of Kathy's favorite ways to finish her wedding cakes and comes from a traditional shaker recipe.

> 3 cups maple syrup
> 3 egg whites (room temperature)
> 1/4 tsp. sea salt

Place the maple syrup in a heavy saucepan (oil the rim of the pan to keep the syrup from overflowing). Attach a candy thermometer and cook until it registers 232°F, stirring occasionally. Beat the egg whites and sea salt together until peaked. As soon as the syrup has reached 232°F, begin to drip it very slowly into the egg whites, beating with an electric mixer for best results. (A hand beater will achieve the same results, but you will need assistance and more time.)

Keep beating until the icing begins to thicken. Lift a little of the icing up with a wooden spoon. When it has a very stiff, threadlike appearance, it is ready.

Ice the cake immediately with a spatula, sweeping it with an upward motion around the sides and top. Decorate with real flowers, nuts, rind, etc.

This recipe will decorate a round four-tier cake. If you prepare a smaller amount, use 1 egg white per cup of maple syrup.

## Carob Frosting

> 1/2 cup concentrated sweetener
> 1/2 cup carob powder
> 1/4 cup tahini
> 1/4 tsp. sea salt
> 1 tsp. anise
> 2 tsp. vanilla

Heat sweetener in a heavy saucepan until warm. Stir in carob powder (sift if lumpy), and continue to cook stirring constantly until just under boiling. Add next three ingredients, stirring as you go. Remove from heat and mix in vanilla. Stir until creamy and smooth. Use immediately for icing, filling or topping. It can also be used as a fudge. If you are using greaseproof paper, oil it first so that the candy or topping doesn't stick.

To use as a cake icing, you may want to add several Tbsp. of liquid for thinning. In this case, add apple juice after salt and cook slightly.

## Glazes

Glazes give cakes or pastries a smooth, shiny appearance. If you want the glaze to drip down the sides of the cake, thin it by adding more liquid (about 2 Tbsp.). If you want to use the glaze as a filling, decrease the liquid. See Fruit Purée II Variations (p. 64), for advice on handling arrowroot flour. Kuzu may be substituted for arrowroot, using slightly more liquid (p. 20). Recipes may also be augmented with natural flavorings, fruits, nuts or seeds.

### Basic Glaze I

> 1 cup cider or any fruit juice
> Pinch of sea salt
> 1 Tbsp. arrowroot flour
> 2 Tbsp. cider or any fruit juice
> 1/4 cup roasted sesame seeds

Heat 1 cup juice or cider and sea salt together in a heavy saucepan; bring to a boil. Dissolve arrowroot flour in 2 Tbsp. cider or fruit juice and add to the boiling liquid, stirring rapidly until it boils again, thickens and turns clear. Remove from heat immediately and stir in seeds. Pour over dessert and serve.

### Basic Glaze II

Follow the recipe for Basic Glaze I, reducing

the cup of juice to 3/4 cup. Substitute 2 Tbsp. tangerine, orange or lemon rind for sesame seeds.

### Variations for Basic Glazes

*Coffee glaze:* Bring apple juice and sea salt to a boil. Before adding arrowroot mixture, add 2–3 Tbsp. grain coffee substitute and boil until coffee dissolves.

*Spice glaze:* Follow directions for Coffee Glaze, adding 1/2–1 tsp. cloves, ginger or cinnamon (or a combination) after cooking. Stir and let sit 2–3 minutes before using.

*Fruit glaze:* Soak 1/4 cup dried fruit in apple juice or cider to cover until soft. Drain and save liquid; add enough liquid to bring to 1 cup. Dice fruit, replace in liquid and boil 10 minutes. Add arrowroot mixture and follow Basic Glaze recipe.

*Fresh fruit glaze:* After cooking, add 1 tsp. lemon rind and 3 cups diced strawberries, blueberries, apples, pears or other fruit. Stir well. (Decrease liquid accordingly.)

*Raisin-orange glaze:* Add 1/2 cup soaked raisins to orange glaze before cooking.

*Pepper-mint glaze:* Place 2 mint-tea bags in 1 cup apple juice and boil. Remove bags, add dissolved arrowroot and stir rapidly. Continue as with Basic Glaze.

*Vanilla glaze:* Add 1 tsp. vanilla extract (or to taste) after removing pan from heat. Or use vanilla bean (see p. 24).

*Nut or seed glaze:* Add 1/2 cup roasted sunflower seeds, almonds, walnuts, pecans, peanuts or chestnuts to glaze after cooking.

*Nut butter glaze:* Blend 2 Tbsp. of any nut butter into juice or cider before cooking. This glaze will not be as clear, but it will still be as shiny.

*Coconut glaze:* Add 1 Tbsp. coconut to glaze after cooking.

## Crumb Glaze

    4 Tbsp. concentrated sweetener

    4 Tbsp. oil
    1 cup cake or cookie crumbs
    1/2 tsp. cinnamon

Combine ingredients and apply to dessert before baking.

## Nut Glaze

    1/4 cup concentrated sweetener
    2 Tbsp. oil
    1 unbeaten egg white
    2 Tbsp. concentrated sweetener
    1/2 cup crushed nuts
    1/2 tsp. cinnamon

Blend first three ingredients together. Add the rest of the ingredients and spread on top of dessert before baking.

**Peppermint** (*Mentha piperita*)
This herb is mostly used for its essential oil, obtained by distilling the fresh plants. The oil is secreted by glands which are often visible to the eye as translucent dots on the leaf of the plant. Also used to make tea, it can be found growing wild in most parts of the United States in the late spring and summer. If used in jelly-type desserts, puddings or custards, it will enhance the flavor of any sweet.

## Almond Glaze

    1 cup almond milk (p. 149)
    Pinch of sea salt
    3/4 Tbsp arrowroot flour
    1-1/2 Tbsp. concentrated sweetener

2 tsp. lemon juice
1–1-1/2 tsp. lemon rind to taste

Heat 3/4 cup almond milk and sea salt together in heavy saucepan over medium heat until boiling. Dilute arrowroot flour in sweetener and 1/4 cup almond milk. Add this to boiling almond milk, stirring constantly, until mixture boils, thickens and turns clearer. Remove from heat, add lemon juice and rind, and stir. Use immediately.

### Variation

*Almond coffee mint glaze:* Follow recipe for Almond Glaze. Add 2–3 Tbsp. grain coffee before boiling and 1/4 tsp. dried mint to almond milk after boiling. If you prefer, cook 2 mint-tea bags in juice or almond milk until liquid boils, add grain coffee and let simmer 2–3 minutes. Then add other ingredients and follow recipe.

**Sweet Potato** (*Convolvulaceae*)
A vegetable of the morning glory family, its large, fleshy roots are a popular food. Juicy sweet potatoes are often called yams, but the yam belongs to another family and grows mostly in the tropics. Sweet potatoes may be yellow or white. The yellow ones grow mostly in the southern United States; white sweet potatoes come from Africa or Asia.

Some kinds of sweet potato plants have pale green vines with green pointed leaves. Others have purple vines with large leaves. The vines grow from the main stem and lie along the ground.

Sweet potatoes first grew in tropical regions of the Western Hemisphere. They were raised in colonial Virginia during the early 1600s. They are sometimes used in making alcohol and starch.

# Purées

## Vegetable Purée I

> 6–8 cups chopped squash, carrots,
> sweet potato, parsnips, pumpkin,
> beets or yams*
> 2 Tbsp. oil
> 1/2 tsp. sea salt
> 2 Tbsp. concentrated sweetener
> (optional)

Chop vegetables into bite-size pieces. (If using squash, pumpkin or yams, remove skins before cooking.) Heat oil in a heavy skillet. Sauté vegetables on a low heat for 5 minutes, stirring occasionally. Add sea salt, cover and cook until tender. Add sweetener if desired. Purée in food mill or blender.

### Alternate Method

Cut squash, pumpkin, sweet potato or yam into thin strips or wedges (like melons). Baste with *tamari* and oil. Heat oven to 350°F. Place in casserole, add water (1/4 inch), cover and bake until tender. Uncover 5 minutes before removing from oven (to allow excess water to evaporate). These vegetables sometimes taste sweeter if baked instead of sautéed.

## Vegetable Purée II

> 2 cups vegetable puree
> 2 Tbsp. tahini, sesame, almond or
> peanut butter
> 2–3 Tbsp. arrowroot flour (see Fruit
> Purée II, p. 64)
> 1/4 cup concentrated sweetener or
> apple juice
> 1 tsp. orange or lemon rind

---

\* Squash, pumpkin and yams contain more liquid, so use a larger quantity of these vegetables.

Prepare vegetable purée; allow to cool.

Place purée and nut butter in a saucepan and cook on a medium flame until mixture boils. Dilute arrowroot in concentrated sweetener or juice. Add arrowroot combination to purée and stir constantly until it comes to a boil and thickens.

Remove from heat. Stir in rind.

### Variations for Vegetable Purées I and II

Combine two different vegetables and/or fruits together in ratios such as:

| | |
|---|---|
| carrot—beet | 3:1 |
| carrot—squash | 1:1 |
| carrot—parsnip | 3:1 |
| apricot—yam | 1:1 |
| beet—parsnip | 1:2 |
| parsnip—yam | 1:2 |
| squash—parsnip | 2:1 |
| pear—parsnip | 2:1 |
| carrot—raisin | 2:1 |

See also variations for Oat Cream (p. 145).

## Chestnut Purée

Chestnut Purée is widely used in European pastries because of its delicate taste and texture.

*To prepare with dried chestnuts:* Soak in liquid to cover overnight. Add more liquid to cover if necessary before cooking. Bring to a boil and then simmer, covered, until tender. Drain off liquid, cool, and purée in a food mill or blender, or mash like potatoes.

*To prepare with fresh chestnuts:* Cut a cross with a knife on the flat side of each chestnut. Place in a saucepan and cover with cold liquid. Bring to a boil.

Remove from heat. Take out chestnuts (a few at a time) and peel off outer and inner skins while warm.

Cover the chestnuts with liquid. Simmer until tender. Drain, reserving liquid. Cool, then mash, blend, or purée in a food mill. Leftover liquid can be used as flavoring in

other desserts.

## Fruit Purée I

1 cup dried apricots
Apple juice or water
1 tsp. vanilla
1/4 tsp. sea salt

Put fruit in a saucepan with enough juice to almost cover. Bring to a boil, lower heat and simmer uncovered until no liquid remains.

Remember that each type of fruit is different; some may require more liquid, some less. Adjust accordingly.

Make a large quantity and keep it refrigerated until you want to use it.

## Fruit Purée II

1-1/2 cups dried fruit
2 Tbsp. arrowroot flour (1 Tbsp. per cup
  of puréed fruit)
1/2 tsp. sea salt

Soak fruit in liquid to cover until soft. Add more liquid if necessary to cover fruit. Simmer in a covered pan 30 minutes.

Strain off extra liquid and set aside. Allow liquid to cool. Purée fruit in a food mill or blender. When liquid is cool, dilute arrowroot flour in 1/2 cup liquid.

Combine arrowroot mixture and sea salt, then purée, adding more liquid if necessary to make 2 cups. Place in a saucepan and cook on a medium heat, stirring constantly until mixture comes to a boil and thickens.

### Variations

To use fresh fruit, follow the recipe for Vegetable Purée (p. 63), substituting fruit for vegetables. When using arrowroot flour, remember quantity needed is 1 Tbsp. per cup of liquid. When you combine arrowroot flour with Fruit or Vegetable Purée, it may be necessary to add a few more Tbsp. of purée or some fruit juice per Tbsp. of arrowroot flour because of the thicker consistency of the purée.

See Oat Cream variations (p. 145) for other suggestions.

Apple Butter may be substituted for any fruit purée.

## Fillings

### Lemon Nut Filling

    3 Tbsp. oil
    1/2 lb. roasted sesame seeds
    3–4 cups roasted almonds
    1/2 cup concentrated sweetener
    1 Tbsp. lemon rind
    1 tsp. cinnamon
    1/4 tsp. sea salt
    1 tsp. lemon juice

Sauté all of ingredients except lemon juice for 5 minutes, mixing occasionally. Remove from heat, add lemon juice, toss lightly.

### Raisin Nut Filling

    2 Tbsp. corn or maize meal or 1 Tbsp.
      bread crumbs
    1-1/2 cups roasted almonds or walnuts
    1/4 cup concentrated sweetener
    1/4 cup tahini
    1/2 cup raisins
    1 tsp. orange or lemon rind
    1/2 tsp. sea salt
    1 tsp. vanilla

Roast flour until lightly browned. Set aside to cool. While still warm, crush the roasted nuts for 30 seconds in a blender or with a mortar and pestle.

Combine roasted flour with concentrated sweetener, stir in chopped nuts, tahini,

raisins, rind, sea salt and vanilla. Use as filling for pastry sheets, tarts, strudels.

### Walnut Filling

    1-1/2 cups roasted chopped walnuts
    1/2 grated apple
    1/2 cup oil
    1/2 cup raisins
    1 tsp. orange rind
    1 tsp. vanilla
    1/4 tsp. sea salt
    1 tsp. cinnamon

Combine the above ingredients. Mix well. Use for pastry sheets, tarts, strudels.

### Almond Nut Filling

    4 cups chopped roasted almonds
    2 tsp. cinnamon
    1 tsp. cardamon
    1-1/2 cups oil
    1/4 tsp. sea salt

Sauté nuts and spices in oil for 5 minutes, stirring occasionally. Cool and fill pastry sheets, tarts, strudels, etc.

### Tofu Crumb Filling

    2 cups tofu
    1/4 tsp. sea salt
    1 beaten egg
    1 tsp. vanilla
    1/4 cup concentrated sweetener or
      1/2 cup Chestnut Cream (p. 144)
    Grated rind of 1/2 lemon or orange
    1/2 cup raisins
    1/4 cup roasted chopped almonds or
      walnuts

Break tofu into small pieces. In a warm skillet, lightly sauté tofu and sea salt. Set aside 5 minutes to cool.

Combine lightly beaten egg, tofu, vanilla,

sweetener, rind and raisins. Mix together until all ingredients are combined. Add nuts. This texture is good for strudels (p. 99).

**Corn or Maize**
Originally a food crop of the Western Hemisphere, corn was taken to Europe by Colombus and has spread all over the temperate zone of the world. It has long been the staple of the American Indians and was supplemented in their diet by beans, sweet potatoes and squash.

The people of Latin America and Southern and Eastern Africa use ground cornmeal. In Latin America, cornmeal is cooked into flat-cakes called *tortillas*; in Africa, it is boiled with water into a cereal resembling the Italian *polenta*.

In the United States, most of the corn crop is grown for livestock feed. But white and yellow cornmeal is commonly used as a cereal; and, as corn flour, it goes into breads, pancake batters and desserts.

## Crumb Topping

*Crumbs*

There are many ways to convert leftover breads, cakes or cookies into crumbs. To dry out, place them on a baking sheet in a 275°F oven before making crumbs. Bake until dry, but not browned. Crush them in a hand mill, or with mortar and pestle, or chop and then roll between two sheets of paper. Substitute crumbs for flour in any of the following recipes.

Any of these crumb topping recipes may be used as fillings, pastry dough, or snacks as well.

## Oat Crumb Topping or Crust

> 1 cup roasted whole wheat flour
> 2 cups rolled oats
> 1/2 cup cornmeal or maize meal
> 2 tsp. cinnamon
> 1/2 tsp. sea salt
> 1/4 cup crushed nuts
> 1/2 cup oil
> 4 Tbsp. maple syrup
> 1 tsp. vanilla
> Apple juice to bind

Combine all dry ingredients together. Beat oil, maple syrup and vanilla together, and combine with dry mixture. Mix until it becomes sticky, adding a few drops of juice if necessary. Do not saturate with too much juice—texture should resemble a crumble. Sprinkle on top of dessert and bake, or sprinkle onto cookie tray and bake, until firm and lightly browned. Cool and store in jar if not using immediately.

This recipe can also be used for a pie crust or biscuits. Add enough apple juice to bind. Press into pre-oiled pan, and bake.

## Coffee Crumb Topping

> 1/2 cup whole wheat flour
> 1 cup rolled oats
> 1/4 cup roasted sesame seeds
> 2 tsp. instant grain coffee
> 1/4 tsp. sea salt
> 1/4 cup oil
> 1/4 cup maple syrup
> 1/4–1/2 cup apple juice or cider

Roast flour until lightly browned. Roast rolled oats until brown. Combine all dry ingredients. Rub oil and sweetener into dry mixture, adding more liquid if necessary.

## Crumb Toppings

　　2 cups rolled oats
　　1/2 cup roasted sesame or chopped
　　　　sunflower seeds
　　2 tsp. cinnamon
　　1 tsp. orange or lemon rind
　　1/2 tsp. sea salt
　　1 tsp. vanilla
　　Apple juice or cider
　　1/4 cup oil

Follow directions for Coffee Crumb Topping.

## Grain Syrup

Pressure-cook or boil 2 cups brown rice without salt, in 5 cups water for 45 minutes. Place in a bowl (not metallic) and cool to 140°F (use a candy thermometer). To the cooked rice, add freshly made grain sprouts* which have been crushed or blended.

　　Cover and keep in a warm place, so that temperature of the rice-sprout mixture is maintained at 130°–140°F for 4–5 hours.

(You can place it on a warm stove, or rest it in a pan of hot water.) Remove cover and taste. If it is not sweet enough, cover and let sit another few hours, tasting often. Squeeze liquid through cheesecloth into pan. Reserve grain for puddings, etc. Add a pinch of sea salt and cook until desired consistency is reached.

**Variation**
For a different texture, do not squeeze liquid through cheesecloth. Blend. This can be used as a warm drink, and be used to sweeten recipes, or over cakes.

---

* Use 1 Tbsp. unsprouted grain to every 1-1/2 cups cooked rice. To make sprouts, use whole oats, barley, wheat or rice. Place in a glass jar, put a cheesecloth over the top of the jar and secure. Soak at least 12 hours in springwater to cover. Drain through cheesecloth, rinse with fresh water and drain again. Lay jar on its side in a warm, dark place. Rinse and drain each day to maintain moisture.

　　The grain will sprout in 3–6 days, depending on the grain used and the temperature; the warmer the temperature, the shorter the time needed.

# 4. SENSIBLE SUSTENANCE: Breads for All Occasions

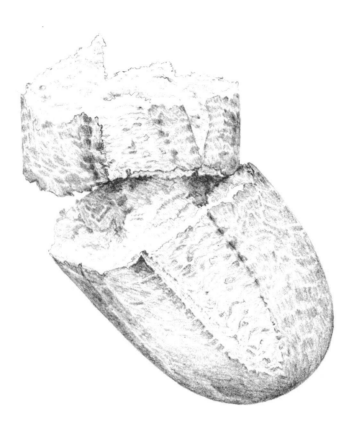

So-called "high fiber breads" and "bran breads" are very popular now because they are promoted with the idea that they are an aid to weight loss. The reason given is that because the so-called "fiber" cannot be digested, it cannot possibly cause weight gain. This is not necessarily true. When digestive systems are not accustomed to eating whole grains or even whole wheat flour products, bread with extra bran can produce flatulence and a bloated feeling. There have been actual instances known when ground wood fiber has been added to the bread instead of extra bran, even though the digestive system of human beings is not able to handle wood pulp.

Phytic acid is a compound that is found mostly in plant foods but especially in beans, peas and whole grains. It has the ability to combine with minerals like iron, calcium and zinc, and form insoluble compounds which are carried out in the stool. So, bread with added bran is not necessarily beneficial to some people.

Phytase, the enzyme responsible for splitting phytic acid in the intestines is available during bread-making: a moist atmosphere and warm temperature have the ability to activate this enzyme and enable it to break down the phytic acid in the various grains.

For a better bread that is easier to digest, follow these easy steps:

1. Always let the bread dough rise two or three times.
2. Add sour grain, apple cider or juice to the dough to create a slightly acidic environment.
3. Eat leavened bread with sour dough starter or yeast.

Man can readily adapt to whole grains without suffering from feelings of flatulence or bloatedness, or mineral deficiency. The phytic acid problem ceases to be a problem usually after several months of eating a diet of whole grains, beans and vegetables. However, there are people who have been known not to be able to deal with excessive quantities of phytic acid and sometimes can suffer from mineral deficiency diseases as a result.

# Forget Me Knots

1. Liquid content will vary according to the temperature of the room, the moisture in the flour and the air, and the general weather conditions of the day.
2. Try using 50 percent whole wheat flour and a combination of other flours such as corn, millet, oats and barley. Buckwheat and rye flour should only comprise about 10 percent of total volume.
3. Use whole wheat flour that is high in gluten for best results. This flour is usually more coarsely ground than pastry flour.
4. You can use 1–3 cups of fermented or freshly cooked grain in addition to the rest of the ingredients (decrease flour by 1/3).
5. Batter loaves are better for warmer weather as they contain more moisture.
6. Place baking tins in warm oven before oiling to allow them to absorb oil.
7. Flour bottom of tin with coarse flour (meal) for best results.
8. Fill tins no more than two thirds full with batter or dough to allow bread to rise *almost* to the top of the tin.
9. Sprinkle seeds on top of bread or in bottom of pan before baking.
10. For kneaded loaf, brush with beaten egg before baking.
11. Place water in the bottom of the oven to create extra moisture. This prevents hard crust from forming on kneaded loaves.
12. Tap bread to see if it baked. It should sound hollow and slightly contract away from the sides of the pan.
13. Allow bread to sit 10 minutes in tin before removing.
14. Place bread, upside-down on rack and wrap in towel until cool. This prevents bread from drying out.
15. For savory loaf, follow any sour-dough recipe. Omit dried fruit and add 1 Tbsp. dried herbs: basil, rosemary or thyme.
16. Cold oven in a recipe refers to one that is *not* preheated.

**Grape** (*Vitis*)
The grape is one of the oldest and most important perennial fruit plants referred to in the Bible. Raisin is the name for dried grapes. The fruit from this species may be consumed fresh, dried for raisins or used for wines.

The important varieties differ in their versatility for these uses. *Sultanini* (Thompson Seedless) and *muscat* are grown in large quantity for all three purposes. The *zante* current is grown only for its raisins.

California dries more than half of its grapes for raisins. Because of their high percentage of fruit sugar, sugar was manufactured from raisins in the early 1900s in practically all the countries of Western Asia and Southern Europe.

# Whole Wheat Sour Dough

## Sour Dough Starter

> 2 cups whole wheat flour
> 2 cups water

Combine flour and water in a bowl. Stir to form a porridge-like mixture that can drop easily from the end of a wooden spoon. Cover and set in a warm place to "ferment." Everyday, stir the mixture and skim off any brown or grey liquid that forms on top; this alcoholic substance can turn moldy. If this occurs, pour away all but 2 Tbsp. and use the remaining "starter" to begin all over again.

At the end of 3–5 days, the mixture should begin to take on a "sour-sweet" smell. This means that the starter is now ready to be used.

If you are not ready to make a bread or cake, then place in covered glass jar and refrigerate until using. The starter should be *fed* at least every seven days. So, if you do not use it within this time, pour off accumulated liquid that has formed on top, stir in 2–3 Tbsp. of whole wheat flour, water, cover, and refrigerate again.

## Sour Dough Raisin Bread

> 1 recipe sour dough starter
> 2–2-1/2 cups water
> 4–4-1/2 cups whole wheat flour, or 50 percent whole wheat and other flours (never use more than 10 percent buckwheat or rye)
> 1 cup chopped sultanas
> 4 Tbsp. roasted crushed sunflower or sesame seeds
> 3/4 tsp. sea salt

Combine starter, 2 cups water, and 2 cups whole wheat flour. Cover and set bowl in a warm place for 30 minutes.

Take 1 cup of this mixture and place in covered jar to replace original "starter." Refrigerate until next bake.

Combine the remaining batter, and the rest of the flour, sultanas, seeds and salt to form the bread batter (adjust liquid-flour content accordingly). The batter should drop with difficulty from a wooden spoon.

Beat batter 10 minutes or until batter becomes stringy. (This will be gluten forming.) Cover and let rest 4–10 hours, or until batter almost doubles in size.

Beat down and continue mixing 10 minutes longer. Heat two bread tins before oiling. Flour bottom with cornmeal, and place enough batter in each tin to fill halfway.

Cover with same size bread tin, set in a warm place and allow to rise almost to the top of the tin (4–10 hours).

Place in cold oven and set temperature to 375°F. Bake 1 hour, lower temperature to 350°F and bake 45–60 minutes longer, or until they sound hollow when tapped. For best results, bake with pan of water on bottom of oven.

## Instant Starter Bread

> 2 Tbsp. miso
> 2–3 Tbsp. water (leftover noodle water)
> 2 cups warm water
> 4–5 cups whole wheat flour
> Any leftover whole grains
> 1 cup chopped dried mixed fruit

Dissolve miso in 2–3 Tbsp. water until creamy. Mix together with the rest of the ingredients. Beat batter 10 minutes. (Adjust liquid content accordingly.) Cover with cloth and keep in a warm place overnight.

The following day, beat down batter and continue beating for 5 minutes.

# Other Breads

## Carrot Bread

> 1/4 cup warm concentrated sweetener
> 3 egg yolks
> 1/2 cup unrefined safflower oil
> 1 cup sifted whole wheat pastry flour
> 1 tsp. cinnamon
> 1/2 tsp. cardamon
> 1/2 tsp. coriander
> 1/2 cup crushed roasted cashews

Add more flour to form a kneadable dough. (This bread may also be a batter bread if desired—then do not add extra flour to form dough.) Knead 10 minutes and shape into loaves.

Oil and flour bread tins. Place in pans, slit top, cover and let rise. When bread almost reaches the top of the tin, place in cold oven, set to 375°F. Bake for 1 hour, then lower temperature to 350°F and bake another 30–45 minutes or until bread sounds hollow when tapped.

## Apple Apricot Spread

> 4 apples
> 1/2 cup sultanas
> 2 cups dried apricots
> 1/2–1 cup apple juice
> 1 tsp. cinnamon
> 1/2 tsp. ginger
> 1/2 tsp. coriander
> 1 Tbsp. miso

Core and chop apples. (Peel if not organic.) Combine apples, sultanas, apricots and enough juice to cover fruit in saucepan. Bring to a boil, add the next four ingredients, cover and simmer 15 minutes. Remove cover and boil off excess liquid. Cream in miso, cool and use as spread on bread.

> 1 Tbsp. lemon rind
> 1 cup grated carrots
> 3 egg whites
> Pinch of sea salt

Beat together warm sweetener and yolks until the mixture resembles thick cream. Slowly drip in the oil and continue beating until fully absorbed.

Sift together the next four ingredients.

Add cashews, rind, carrots and fold into first mixture.

Beat egg whites with sea salt till stiff peaks form. Gently fold about 1/3 of the egg whites into the batter and then add remaining whites to batter, folding gently.

Bake in oiled and floured baking pan with shallow sides in 350°F degree preheated oven 45–50 minutes or till bread tests done. Turn off oven and leave door slightly ajar. Leave bread there until cool. Remove from pan and when completely cool, cut and serve.

This bread does not come out as high as a conventional bread. If you wish a higher loaf, use a yeast starter and double the recipe. (See p. 104 for "Working with Yeast.")

**Bread Wheat** (*Triticum aestivum*)
This type comprises many different kinds of wheats such as spring wheat (grown in the spring and harvested in the late summer), winter wheat (planted in the fall and harvested in the early summer), hard wheats and soft wheats. They are a main source of flour for making cakes and pastry. Bread wheat is grown in many places, including America, Russia, Asia and Europe.

## Sprouted Wheat Bread

> 3 cups lukewarm apple juice
> 1-1/2 Tbsp. dry yeast
> 1/4 cup concentrated sweetener
> 3 Tbsp. corn oil
> 1 tsp. sea salt

> 2 cups (ground or mashed) wheat berry sprouts
> 4 cups whole meal flour
> Whole wheat pastry flour

Dissolve yeast in a few Tbsp. juice until creamy. Add the sweetener, cover and set aside in a warm place until bubbly. Add the rest of the ingredients, adding enough whole wheat pastry flour to make a smooth, soft dough that is not too sticky. Knead well until smooth and elastic—adding flour and oiling hands to keep from sticking. Place in oiled and floured tins. Cover and let rise until almost doubled. Bake in preheated 350°F oven for 1 hour or until bread pulls away from the sides of the pan and sounds hollow when tapped. Remove from pan and cool.

## New Year's Sweet Bread

The Italian people have known about sweet bread since it was first introduced (according to Dante) in the eastern part of Italy by a merchant named Niccolo Salimbeni. One of the most famous sweet breads known throughout the world is *Panforte*, originally named Honey Spice Bread. It was a favorite among the popes and kings as early as the twelfth century, and is a traditional sweet bread for Christmas and New Years.

> 1/2 lb. mixed dried fruit
> 1–2 cups hard cider or 1/2 Guinness and 1/2 cider
> 1 cup roasted almonds
> 1 cup roasted hazelnuts
> 1 cup whole wheat pastry flour
> 1 tsp. cinnamon
> 1/2 tsp. cloves
> 1 tsp. ginger
> 1/2 tsp. salt
> 1/2 cup concentrated sweetener
> 3–4 Tbsp. instant grain coffee
> 2 Tbsp. orange rind

2 Tbsp. lemon rind
1 tsp. vanilla

Oil and lightly flour loaf tin.

Soak dried fruit in cider to cover until soft. Squeeze out excess liquid and reserve juice. Dice fruit.

Combine next seven ingredients in mixing bowl. Set aside.

Bring the concentrated sweetener and instant grain coffee to a boil, simmer covered 5 minutes. Add rinds and vanilla.

Combine both mixtures together, adding enough of the reserved liquid until a thick batter is formed.

Place in oiled tin, cover and bake in 300°F oven 20 minutes. Remove cover, and bake 30–40 minutes longer or until bread pulls away from the sides of the tin.

Brush with concentrated sweetener immediately after removing from pan. Cool on rack before cutting.

## Sultana and Cashew Loaf

1 Tbsp. dry yeast
1/2 cup warm apple juice
2 Tbsp. whole wheat flour
1/2 cup sultanas
Water or juice to almost cover sultanas
1/2 cup safflower or corn oil
1/2 cup concentrated sweetener
2 eggs (room temperature)
1/2 cup Tofu Sour Cream (p. 147)
1/2 cup roasted chopped cashews
1/2 cup roasted sesame seeds
1/2 tsp. sea salt
1 Tbsp. cinnamon
1 Tbsp. grated orange rind
2 cups whole wheat flour

Combine first three ingredients. Cover and set aside to rise. Combine next two ingredients, cover and bring to a boil. Lower heat and simmer until tender. Remove cover and cook down until there is no excess liquid. Place sweetener in bowl and slowly drip in oil while beating. Beat in first two mixtures. Add eggs, one at a time and continue to beat. Gradually incorporate Tofu Sour Cream and next five ingredients. Sift in flour and fold into batter. (Consistency should be thick but dropable.) Oil and flour two loaf tins. Pour into pans and cover, set aside to rise. Bake in preheated 325°F oven 50–60 minutes or until wooden skewer inserted in center is withdrawn clean.

## Onion and Sesame Loaf

1-1/2 Tbsp. dry yeast
1/4 cup apple juice
2 Tbsp. buckwheat flour
2 egg yolks
1/2 cup concentrated sweetener
1/4 cup unrefined safflower oil
2 Tbsp. oil
2 cups chopped onion
1/2 tsp. sea salt
1/2 cup brown rice flour
1/4 cup buckwheat flour minus 2 Tbsp.
1/2 cup maize flour
1/2 cup roasted sesame seeds
2 egg whites

Combine first three ingredients. Cover and set aside to rise. In a separate bowl, combine next three ingredients and beat until smooth and creamy. Drip in oil while constantly beating.

Heat skillet, add oil and sauté onion until clear and lightly browned. Sprinkle in sea salt and remove from skillet. Combine first two mixtures and remaining ingredients except egg whites lightly with sautéed onions. (You may have to add 1/4 cup apple juice if mixture is too thick.) Beat egg whites with a pinch of salt until peaked. Mix one third of egg whites into batter and then fold in the remaining two thirds of egg whites very gently. Place in oiled and floured pan's two thirds full, cover and rise. Bake in a preheated 350°F oven 40–50 minutes or until skewer inserted in center pulls out clean. Place on rack to cool.

## Orange Raisin Bread

    1 Tbsp. dry yeast
    1–2 cups apple cider or juice
    2 cups whole wheat pastry flour
    1/4 cup oil
    2 cups soaked raisins
    2 Tbsp. orange, tangerine or lemon rind
    1/2 tsp. sea salt

Dissolve yeast in 1 cup warm apple juice or cider. Stir and set aside for a few minutes, until it bubbles. Add enough flour to form a thin batter, beating with a wooden spoon. Cover and set in a warm place to rise until doubled in size.

Combine the rest of the ingredients with the yeasted batter, adding more apple juice until soft dough is formed. Knead for 10 minutes.

Oil a loaf pan. Place dough in pan. Cover and let rise in warm spot until almost double.

Preheat oven to 350°F. Bake 45–55 minutes or until bread sounds hollow when tapped, and pulls away from the sides of the pan.

## Pumpkin Bread

    1/4 cup oil
    2 cups grated pumpkin
    1 cup roasted chopped nuts
    1 cup whole wheat bread crumbs
    1 tsp. cloves
    1 tsp. cinnamon
    1 Tbsp. mint
    1/2 cup whole wheat pastry flour
    3 egg yolks
    1/4 cup concentrated sweetener
    Rind and juice of 1 orange

**Squash** (*Cucurbitaceae*)
The squash, cucumber, melon and pumpkin are all members of the same family. They are all trailing or climbing herbs, with tendrils and large, lobed leaves. The flowers are usually yellow and the berry-like fruit is generally oval or round in shape.

The most familiar kind of pumpkin grown in northern America is usually orange, maturing in October just before Halloween. Another kind of pumpkin, called *natawari* (from the Japanese for "to split with an axe") was first grown in Hokkaido, a northern island of Japan. Unlike its relative, it is greenish-blue on the outside and deep yellow on the inside. This type of pumpkin is now in some parts of the eastern United States, maturing at the same time as the "Halloween pumpkin." It has a strong, sweet taste that is excellent for the traditional pumpkin pie.

Some squash varieties that are good in desserts are butternut, buttercup, acorn and winter squash. Most of these squash are very sweet if used in season.

    2 Tbsp. sesame butter
    1/2 tsp. sea salt
    3 egg whites

Heat skillet. Sauté pumpkin in oil quickly. Remove from pan.

Combine pumpkin with next six ingredients. Beat yolks and sweetener together until creamy and light. Add next two ingredients, and continue beating 2–3 minutes.

Whisk salt and whites together until stiff peaks form.

Combine pumpkin mixture with yolks. Mix well. Fold in whites gently, until no longer visible. Adjust liquid content accordingly (should be batter-like).

Preheat oven to 350°F. Oil bottom of loaf pan. Flour. Spoon into pan. Bake 45–60 minutes or until bread pulls away from the sides of the pan. Turn off oven, leave door slightly ajar and cool before removing.

## Salty Wheat Sticks

> 1-1/2 Tbsp. dry yeast
> 1 tsp. concentrated sweetener or apple
>     juice
> 1-1/2 cups lukewarm water
> 3 cups whole wheat bread flour (high
>     gluten)
> 1 Tbsp. miso
> 2 Tbsp. corn oil
> Extra oil
> Crude sea salt

Dissolve yeast and sweetener in water; let stand until bubbly. Make a well in the center of the flour, pour half of the yeast mixture into well, and mix. Stir in miso, oil and remaining yeast mixture to form a sticky dough.

Place on floured surface and knead, adding more flour if necessary to form a soft dough. Knead until smooth and elastic—about 10 minutes. Cover and let rise in oiled bowl until doubled in size (30–40 minutes).

Punch down dough; knead briefly. Let rise covered in bowl until doubled—about 30–40 minutes.

Preheat oven to 425°F. Oil baking sheets and sprinkle with crude sea salt. Punch down dough, and divide into 24 pieces. Roll each piece into 12 × 1/2-inch log. Place about 1 inch apart on baking sheets. Brush with oil; sprinkle with salt. Bake until crisp and light brown, about 20–30 minutes. Cool on rack.

This dough can also be used for pizza. Place round of dough on center of pizza tray and press out shape with oiled fingers. Bake without topping until almost done, then top and reheat.

## Breads of Different Shapes

Using recipe for salty wheat sticks, you can shape breads into many different and delightful forms.

Divide dough into three; shape into balls. Flatten balls with palms of hands; roll into 7-inch circles. Roll up each circle tightly into a log. Let rest covered 5 minutes. Roll each log into 12 × 3-inch rectangle. Cover and sprinkle baking sheet with cornmeal. Choose one of the following:

*Artichoke bread*
1. Cut 2-inch slits, spaced 1/2 inch apart, along one long side of one dough rectangle.
2. Starting at short end, roll up dough; pinch seam.
3. Place rolled dough, cut side up on baking sheet.
4. Fold out petals

*Scroll Bread*
1. Roll up two short ends of one dough rectangle toward center, pinching middle of each roll with thumb as you roll and leave 1-inch space between rolls (see illustration).

2. Twist one roll 90°, place on top of other roll.
3. Press center firmly to hold shape.
4. Let rolls stand uncovered 10 minutes or until almost doubled in size.
5. Brush breads lightly with water and bake 15 minutes in 450°F oven, lower heat to 400°F, and bake until golden brown.

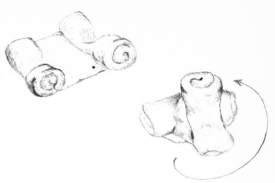

# 5. SHAPING SIMPLY: Pastries, Tarts and Pies

"Delicious . . . fragrant . . . a crust so flaky that it melts in your mouth." These and many more compliments from friends and family will surround you when you have baked pastries from among the recipes that follow.

## Preparing the Dough

*Methods for Adding the Oil*

Choose one of the following:
1. Drip the oil into the dry ingredients in a spiral motion. Using two metal utensils (knives, forks or spoons), cut into the dry mixture until it resembles tiny bread crumbs.
2. Drip oil into dry ingredients in a spiral motion. Rub oil in with your hands

until it looks like tiny bread crumbs.

3. Drip oil into dry ingredients in a spiral motion. Mix with an electric mixer, but only until the flour resembles tiny bread crumbs.

4. Beat liquid and oil together. Add to the dry ingredients, mixing as you go until a ball of pastry is formed.

### Rolling Out

Choose a table which is a comfortable height, neither too low so that you must bend over, nor too high so that you cannot give the rolling pin proper weight.

*Temperature of the dough:* If the dough is too cold (especially oily dough), it may be too hard to roll out. If the dough is too warm, it may be too soft to shape. The dough should be firm when you press your finger into it, but should not stick.

For oily dough, roll out, shape, place in pan, cover and chill 30 minutes before baking. For non-oily pastry, wrap and chill 30 minutes before rolling and shaping.

*Method:* Cover the rolling surface with canvas, muslin cloth, or greaseproof paper large enough to hang over the sides. Flour lightly with arrowroot. (Arrowroot flour is good to use when the pastry is thin and delicate. It helps to keep the dough from tearing or splitting.) If you over-flour the surface, the pastry may become tough and hard to work with.

1) Shape dough into the desired form with your hands before rolling out.

2) Divide dough into several pieces if necessary. Cover and set aside until ready to roll out.

3) Place dough in center of cloth or rolling surface so that there is plenty of room for expansion.

4) Sprinkle the top of the dough and rolling pin with flour.

5) Roll from the center outward with quick, light, short strokes, not pressing too hard. Rotate the dough occasionally.

6) Lift the dough occasionally with a spatula or your hand and flour underneath it lightly to prevent it from sticking.

7) Roll out the dough to desired shape and thickness, 2 inches larger than the size of the form.

*Alternate method:* Lay a piece of grease-proof paper over the rolling surface. Divide dough, shape, cover with paper, roll out into the desired shape and size.

### Transferring Pastry Dough to Pie Pan

*A.* After rolling out pastry dough to desired shape and size, roll one third of it around the rolling pin and lift into the pie pan. Allow pastry dough to fall naturally. Do not stretch pastry, otherwise the dough will shrink during baking.

Be sure that the pastry dough overlaps the edge of the pie pan 1 to 2 inches to form a decorative edge (see p. 81).

*B.* After rolling out pastry dough to desired shape and size between pieces of greaseproof paper, peel off the top layer of paper and invert pastry dough onto the pie pan. Peel off the bottom layer of paper. Allow the dough to drop naturally into pan. Do not stretch it.

# Techniques for Pies and Tarts

### Section Pie or Tart I

For 4-section pie or tart, cut a long strip of dough and roll it into a rope.

1) Use this rope to divide the shell into four sections. Secure it to the bottom crust by brushing with cold liquid.

2) Chill 15 minutes.

3) Bake at 425°F 10 minutes, and 350°F 10 to 15 minutes longer.

4) Fill and serve, or fill after baking 10 minutes with different-colored purées and fillings, return to oven and bake 10 to 15 minutes longer at 350°F or until firm and golden brown.

### Section Pie or Tart II

When filling a prebaked pie shell with cream and/or fruit, reserve half of the filling for the topping.

1) Divide the pie into six or eight slices. Do not cut through.

2) Place cream in a pastry bag and squeeze out design on each alternate slice, leaving every other side empty.

3) Spoon fruit mixture on the remaining sections.

4) Chill before serving.

## Fancy Covers for Pies and Tarts

### Lattice tops

Cut plain strips 1/2 inch wide and 3–4 inches longer than the pie shell. Roll then twist 1/2-inch rope-like pieces. Place them crisscross or weave them together.

### Full cover

Fold the pastry top in half. Cut one pattern on the fold with a small cookie cutter. (This allows steam to escape.) Place top crust over pie, unfold, seal edges, glaze and bake.

### Fancy free

Roll out excess pastry dough to 1/4-inch thickness. With a cookie cutter, glass bowl or cup, cut out several pieces (six or seven, depending upon the size of the cutters and pie) to cover the top of the pie. Lay the pieces over the filling touching each other (try a yeasted dough with this technique). Seal the edges.

## Making Edges for Pie and Tart Crusts

1. Make an attractive edge by pressing the back of a spoon or fork around the edge of the pie.

2. Press the prongs of a fork around the edge of the pie.

3. *Fluted:* Double the edge of the crust. Use your index finger or the handle of a knife to make the indentations, and the thumb and index finger of your other hand as a wedge to push against, making scallops.

4. *Crisscross:* Trim the crust at the edge of the pan. Cut the rolled pastry into 1/2-inch-wide strips. Moisten the edge of the pastry in the pan. Interlace two strips on the edge of the pie. Keep the strips flat, do not twist, turn over or stretch them. To seal, press rounded edge on both sides of crisscrossed strip tightly against moistened edge with your finger.

## Finished Look

For added color in yeasted or unyeasted pastry, brush with egg white, yolk or whole egg, combined with 1 tsp. of cold water, before baking.

For a hard crust and shiny look, brush with any glaze (p. 61) or concentrated sweetener several times while baking, or brush with juice or concentrated sweetener immediately after removing pastry from the oven.

For a clear glaze just before the pastry has finished baking, brush with 1/4 cup concentrated sweetener (dissolve in a small amount of liquid if too thick to apply).

After glazing with any of the above, decorate with crushed roasted nuts.

## Baking a Single Unfilled Pie Crust

There are two ways to bake an unfilled pie shell:

1.  Prick the pastry shell with a fork all over before baking. This allows steam to escape, and prevents the bottom from rising or buckling. The crust will be more evenly browned this way, but also may be more distorted because of the steam.

2.  The second way produces a more evenly shaped pie crust, but the bottom does not brown as much as the rim. Place a large piece of brown paper on the crust. Fill the paper with enough uncooked, oiled rice or beans to hold paper in place. Bake in 375°F oven 12–15 minutes or until crust browns lightly. This will prevent the crust from puffing up. Remove the paper and beans or rice a few minutes before the crust is done.

# Forget Me Knots

1. The amount of liquid and oil necessary for the proper consistency of each recipe will vary according to the moisture and temperature of the flour and the room, the size of the eggs, and the general weather of the day. Remain flexible, and adjust liquid and oil content accordingly.

2. When preparing an unyeasted pastry dough, handle it as little and as delicately as possible. This will inhibit the development of gluten and prevent the dough from becoming tough. Never knead it. After combining all the ingredients with a wooden spoon, lightly shape it into the desired form with your hands before rolling it out.

3. Whole wheat pastry flour makes the most tender pastry dough.

4. Use corn or corn-germ oil for a lighter, more delicate dough.

5. For flakier pastry doughs, liquids and oils should be cold when used, because cold ingredients tend to expand more quickly in the heat of the oven, helping the pastry to be light and flaky.

6. Apple juice, cider, mu tea, mint tea or equal parts juice and tea may be used interchangeably for liquid in any recipe. The resulting pastry may be less sweet.

7. When rolling out a thin, delicate pastry dough, sprinkle arrowroot flour before rolling to prevent the pastry from splitting or tearing.

8. Cut pie dough at least 2 inches larger than pie pan to allow for shrinkage and edges.

9. Chilling dough after rolling prevents shrinkage during baking.

10. Fill a baked shell with a filling of the same temperature, or slightly warmer; otherwise, the shell may crack.

11. Bake pies in oven-glass pie plates or dull metal pans for browner crusts.

12. When completely prebaking a pie shell, prick the bottom and sides with a fork before baking to allow the steam to escape, and oil the rim of the crust to prevent burning.

13. If the filling is juicy, before baking lightly brush the bottom crust with an egg white mixed with a few drops of water or a kuzu-water paste (dilute kuzu to pastry consistency). This will prevent the crust from becoming soggy from the filling.

14. Roll a small tube of wax or heavy paper and insert it into a slit in the center of the top crust of a fruit pie to carry out the steam and prevent the juices from leaking out.

15. One and one-half cups flour will make a single pie crust; 3 cups will make a double-crust pie (8 inches).

16. Four cups of filling are necessary to fill a 8-inch pie shell.

17. For a lighter-colored crust, place a sheet of paper over the pie crust the last 10 minutes of baking time.

18. To make the pastry dough light and puffy when deep-frying, add 1 or 2 tsp. lemon or orange juice, brown rice vinegar or apple cider vinegar to the pastry dough before adding liquid.

# Recipes

## Delicate Pastries

### Baklava

Baklava was created by the Persians, who originally had a nut filling scented with pussy-willow blossoms or jasmine inside the pastry.

Around the sixth century, the Greeks discovered the art of making fine, thin pastry (phylo) and adopted Baklava as their traditional New Year's dessert.

The only way I found to make the dough thin enough was by using a hot water pastry dough.

HOT WATER PASTRY DOUGH
    2/3 cup oil
    1 tsp. sea salt
    1-1/2 cups apple juice or cider, mu tea or mint tea
    4 cups whole wheat pastry flour
SYRUP:
    1/2 cup oil
    4–6 Tbsp. concentrated sweetener
    2 tsp. cinnamon
    Grated rind of 1 orange
    Grated rind of 1 lemon
    Juice of 1 lemon (1 Tbsp.)
FILLING:
    3 cups crushed walnuts
    1 Tbsp. plus 1 tsp. cinnamon
    1 tsp. dried mint
    Pinch of sea salt

*Hot water pastry dough*
Heat oil, salt and liquid together. Remove from heat and beat by hand for a few minutes. Add this to flour and knead until a soft, sticky dough is formed. Knead about 5 minutes longer, cover and set aside about 30 minutes.

Cut dough into five pieces, the size of an orange, dip in arrowroot flour, cover and let sit in a warm place 1/2 hour.

*Syrup*
Place oil in saucepan and cook on a medium heat. Add cinnamon, rind and bring to a boil. Turn off heat, add lemon juice and cool.

*Filling*
Mix together walnuts, cinnamon, salt and mint. Set aside.

*Preparing the pastry*
Sprinkle rolling surface with arrowroot. Roll out pastry on greaseproof paper very, very thin. (It should be almost transparent when held up to the light.) You should have five layers. Set three layers aside for top.

Place two layers of pastry in bottom of rectangular baking pan. Baste in between with oil. Sprinkle some of the walnut mixture over it.

Take the three layers that were set aside and brush olive oil in between each layer. Place on top of the filled pastry.

With a sharp knife, cut crisscross into the top layer. This will allow the top to bake more evenly, as well as decorate it.

Pour the cooled syrup over the pastry before baking. Preheat the oven to 375°F and bake 30–45 minutes or until top is browned and crisp.

### Apple Dumplings

    Strudel Pastry (p. 99)
    6 apples
    1 cup raisins
    1/2 tsp. sea salt
    1/2 cup tahini, almond or peanut butter
    1–2 tsp. cinnamon
    1–2 cups apple juice or cider

Prepare pastry dough; cover and set aside. Peel and core apples. Mix raisins and salt. Stuff the apples half full with raisins. Fill to the top with tahini. Sprinkle tops with cinnamon.

Roll out pastry 1/4 inch thick and cut into six squares large enough to cover a whole apple. Set an apple on each piece of pastry. Wrap pastry around apple, covering it completely.

Score top. Place dumplings in deep oiled pan. Cover and chill 20 minutes.

Preheat oven to 350°F. Spoon 1 or 2 Tbsp. juice or cider over top of each dumpling and bake, basting every 10 minutes with apple juice or cider until browned.

Top with Tofu Cream (p. 147) before serving.

**Variation**

Substitute peaches, pears or apricots (whole or slices), for apples. Do not score top. Heat oil and deep-fry until browned (p. 16).

## Cannoli

This is a famous old Italian delicacy passed down from generation to generation. Here is my version of this delightful dessert.

> 3 cups sifted whole wheat pastry flour
> 1 tsp. cinnamon
> 1/2 tsp. sea salt
> 2 Tbsp. oil
> 2 eggs
> 1/4 cup concentrated sweetener
> 1 tsp. lemon or orange juice, or apple cider vinegar*
> Oil for deep-frying (p. 16)
> Tofu-Cream filling (p. 147)

Sift flour, cinnamon and salt together, into a mixing bowl. Cut in oil. Beat eggs, add sweetener, lemon or orange juice, or vinegar. Stir into dry mixture, and knead until dough is smooth (adjust flour-liquid content accordingly).

Sprinkle arrowroot flour on pastry cloth or wooden surface and roll out dough until very thin. Cut into 4–5-inch ovals or circles.

Fold dough over 1 × 5-inch wooden or metal cylindrical form, and press the ends together in the *center only* as if sealing an envelope. Do not overlap too far. (If ends do not stick together, brush with water or egg yolk before pressing together.)

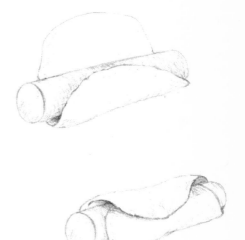

Heat oil. Deep-fry until delicately brown. (Forms may separate from cannolis. Remove them immediately from oil.) Drain and cool. Remove form.

Fill with Tofu Cream just before serving.

Unfilled cannolis may be kept in a cool dry place for several days before using.

---

* Lemon juice, orange juice or vinegar makes the pastries puff up while being deep-fried.

# Eclairs

    1/2 cup oil
    1 cup apple juice or cider
    1 cup sifted whole wheat pastry flour
    1/4 tsp. sea salt
    4 eggs
TOPPING
    Carob Frosting (p. 61)
FILLING I
    2–3 cups Tofu Whip Cream (p. 147)

Combine oil and juice in saucepan. Cook on a medium heat until boiling. Lower heat and add sifted flour and sea salt, continuously stirring until a ball forms in pan.

Remove from heat and add 3 eggs (one at a time), beating after each addition. Beat the last egg, and add it to the mixture slowly. Preheat oven to 425°F. Fill a pastry bag with batter. Squeeze out eclair shape onto oiled baking tray.

Bake for 20–25 minutes. Turn off oven, open door and leave 10–15 minutes longer, otherwise the rapid change in temperature may cause them to fall and become soggy. Slit the side of the pastry open with scissors to allow steam to escape. Allow to cool.

Whip the cream filling. Fill pastry bag with cream and squeeze into eclairs just before serving (use a tube with a large opening).

Prepare Carob Frosting. Top before serving.

# Apple Tofu Delight

    1 recipe Eclair
    2–3 cups Tofu Cream (p. 147)
    1 apple, thinly sliced
    2 tsp. cinnamon
    1/2 cup sliced almonds

Preheat oven to 375°F. Oil and lightly flour a 7-inch circle on a baking sheet. Spread a thin layer of Eclair pastry (about 1/4 inch thick) within the outline of the circle. Spoon remaining pastry around the layer to make a border, or use a pastry bag instead of a spoon (p. 57). Bake in a preheated 425°F oven 20–25 minutes.

Spoon Tofu Cream into the center of the shell. Spread over pastry. Arrange apple slices (peel if not organic) on top of cream. Sprinkle cinnamon on top of apples, and almonds on top of cinnamon. Bake 10 minutes longer.

**Variation**
Substitute Chestnut Cream (p. 144) for Tofu Cream.

# French Crullers

    1/4 cup concentrated sweetener
    1/4 cup oil
    1/2–3/4 cup boiling apple cider or juice
    1/2 tsp. sea salt
    1-1/2 cups sifted whole wheat pastry
      flour
    2 eggs
    1 tsp. vanilla
    Oil for deep-frying (p. 16)

Combine sweetener, oil, juice and salt in a heavy saucepan. Bring to a boil on a medium heat, stirring occasionally. Sift flour and add to pan all at once, stirring quickly, until thickened.

Remove from heat, add eggs immediately, one at a time, beating thoroughly after each addition. Add vanilla. Consistency should be that of a very thick, heavy batter. Adjust flour-liquid content accordingly.

Fill pastry bag (p. 57). Oil wax paper. Squeeze batter onto paper in the shape of circles. Heat oil, drop crullers in by turning paper at an angle or upside-down so that they slide off. Fry until browned, and drain.

Dip into roasted chestnut flour, coconut or cinnamon after frying.

# Horns I

    3 cups whole wheat pastry flour
    1 cup corn flour
    1 tsp. cinnamon
    1/2 tsp. salt
    1/4 cup cold oil
    Apple juice, or any fruit juice or water
        to form soft, firm dough
    3–4 cups Tofu Whip Cream (p. 147)

Sift all dry ingredients. Cut oil in gradually until mixture resembles tiny bread crumbs. Combine liquid with mixture until dough is formed.

    Roll out pastry 1/8 inch thick on arrowroot flour.

    Oil horn-shaped forms. For a 5-inch form, the dough should be 4–5 times as long. Wind each strip around a form, starting at the narrowest end, slightly overlapping the edges. Wind the dough around form until it is 1/2 inch from the top. This space will allow you to remove the form easily after baking.

    *Do not stretch the pastry as you roll it around the tube; this will cause it to shrink and break while baking.*

Cover and chill dough 30 minutes.
Preheat the oven to 350°F. Place the horns on an oiled baking sheet. Bake 45 minutes, or until browned. Remove from oven and cool slightly before removing horns (twist to remove).

    Before serving, prepare pastry bag with your favorite cream filling and fill (p. 57).

# Horns II

Follow recipe for Horns I, substituting Yeasted Pastry. Wind dough around horns. Cover and set in a warm place to rise until it is one third larger. Bake at 350°F for 30–40 minutes, or until lightly browned.

# Horns III

Follow recipe for Horns I. Add 2 tsp. lemon or orange juice, or vinegar to liquid before combining it with dry mixture.

    Heat oil for deep-frying (p. 16). Deep-fry horns until lightly browned. Drain and cool. Remove forms.

# Teiglach

Adapted from a traditional Jewish recipe my mother always used.

    2 cups whole wheat pastry flour
    1/4 tsp. ginger
    1/4 tsp. salt
    2 eggs
    2 Tbsp. oil
    Raisins and nuts (optional)
    Apple juice or cider
GINGER SYRUP:
    1 cup concentrated sweetener
    2 tsp. ginger

Sift flour, 1/4 tsp. ginger and salt together. Place in a mixing bowl. Add eggs, oil, raisins, nuts and enough apple juice or cider to form a soft dough.

    Roll dough into a log, and cut into 1/2-inch pieces.

*Syrup*

Combine sweetener and ginger in a heavy saucepan, and bring to a boil. Drop pieces of dough in, cover and simmer about 30 minutes. Stir occasionally for even browning; cook until all are browned. Inside should be crisp and dry.

Remove from heat and add 2 Tbsp. boiling water to pan to keep Teiglach from sticking. Remove from pan and place on a large sheet or platter so they are not touching. Roll in cinnamon, roasted chestnut flour, coconut or roasted crushed nuts or seeds.

# Crepes

## Basic Crepes

POPPY SEED FILLING
    1/3 cup poppy seeds
    2/3 cup raisins
    1 cup apple juice or cider
    1/4 tsp. sea salt
    1 tsp. vanilla
    1 tsp. orange rind
CREPE BATTER
    2 cups roasted whole wheat pastry flour
    1/4 tsp. sea salt
    Apple juice to form batter
    Oil for pan

*Poppy seed filling*

Cook first four ingredients in an uncovered saucepan for 10 to 15 minutes, or until most of the liquid has evaporated. Blend with vanilla and orange rind until creamy.

*Crepe batter*

Combine flour and salt. Add juice to form thin pancake-like batter. Let sit overnight for best results.

Heat oil in skillet. When oil is very hot (test by dropping a bit of batter into skillet —when it sizzles, it is ready), using a ladle, spoon just enough batter into the pan to cover the bottom. Move pan around quickly in a circular motion until bottom of pan is completely covered with batter. Cook on a medium heat until holes begin to appear on the surface of the crepe.

Remove crepe by turning pan upside-down and flipping crepe onto a cloth. Fill immediately and serve. (Place filling in center, fold both ends toward the center, overlapping, and fasten with a toothpick.)

# Pies: Sweet and Savory

## Apple Pie

EASY DOUBLE CRUST DOUGH
    2-1/2 cups whole wheat pastry flour
    1/2 cup brown rice flour
    1/4 tsp. sea salt
    1/2 tsp. cinnamon
    1 tsp. ginger
    2–3 Tbsp. instant grain coffee (or to taste)
    1/2 cup cold apple juice, cider or water
    1/2 cup cold oil
    1/2 tsp. vanilla
    1 egg white mix with 1 tsp. water
FILLING:
    8–10 cups chopped apples*
    1 tsp. cinnamon
    1/2 tsp. sea salt or 1 Tbsp. miso
    3–4 Tbsp. arrowroot flour
    1/4 cup apple juice or cider
    1 egg yolk

Combine pastry flour, brown rice flour, salt, spices and grain coffee in a mixing bowl. Set aside. Mix liquid, oil and vanilla together.

Slowly add liquid mixture to dry combination, mixing with a wooden spoon until a ball of dough begins to form. Press to-

---

* When using dried fruit, soak in liquid to cover until soft. Measure fruit after soaking.

gether with your hands. Divide dough into two pieces. Keep one piece covered with a damp cloth.

Preheat oven to 375°F. Oil a pie pan and line with pastry; baste with egg white.

Chop fruit (peel if not organic). Combine fruit, spice and salt. Dissolve arrowroot flour in juice or cider and stir until well combined. Pour arrowroot mixture over fruit mixture and toss. Let sit about 10 minutes.

Place filling in pie shell, pilling up fruit in the shape of a pyramid.

Roll out top crust. Cover and secure edge. Prick top crust (p. 82). Glaze with egg yolk.

Bake at 375°F for 15 minutes, lower temperature to 350°F and bake 30 minutes longer, or until fruit is soft. (Test center of pie with a toothpick.)

## Instant Apple Pie

Roll out bottom crust. Brush with egg white and prebake.

Follow measurements for Apple Pie.

Cook fruit and spices together until soft. Use more fruit as the liquid will evaporate.

When the fruit is almost tender, dilute 1 Tbsp. kuzu (p. 20) for every 1-1/4 cups of cooked fruit in 1/2 cup apple juice. (The more liquid or acid that the fruit filling contains, the more kuzu will be needed to thicken the fruit.)

Stir into fruit mixture and cook, stirring continuously, until fruit filling thickens and turn clearer.

Place in warm pie shell and allow to set before cutting.

## Apricot Cream Pie

 1 recipe Nut Pie Crust (p. 93)
 3 cups Tofu Cream (p. 147) or Chestnut
  Cream (p. 144)
 1 cup Apricot Purée (p. 64)

 1/2 cup Crumb Topping (p. 66)

Preheat oven to 375°F. Prepare pastry dough. Prebake shell 10 minutes.

Lower oven temperature to 350°F. Pour the cream into shell. Cover with purée. Sprinkle with Crumb Topping.

Bake 15–20 minutes or until set.

### Alternate Method

Combine purée and cream. Pour into half-baked shell. Bake until set.

**Parsnip** (*Pastinaca sativa*)
This strong yellowish-white root vegetable is found in most parts of the United States as well as Europe. Cultivated since Roman times, it contains large quantities of sugar and starch and has been used for feeding man as well as livestock. If used sparingly in desserts, it will enhance the flavor of any dish.

## Bulgur Parsnip Pie (Savory)

 1 cup uncooked bulgur wheat
 4 Tbsp. oil
 3 cups apple juice or cider
 1/2 tsp. sea salt
 1 cup diced parsnips
 1 grated apple
 1 recipe Pressed Pastry (p. 92)
 Crushed roasted nuts

Roast bulgur wheat in 2 Tbsp. oil until lightly browned. Boil cider. Add salt and bulgur. Reduce heat, cover and cook 15 minutes.

Dice parsnips. Sauté in 2 Tbsp. oil. Cover and cook until soft.

Grate 1 apple. (Peel if not organic.) Purée parsnips and bulgur together. Add grated apple.

Prepare pie crust. Preheat oven to 375°F. Oil a pie pan. Press crust into pan and prebake 10 minutes.

Spread bulgur-parsnip mixture in shell and bake 10 minutes longer. Sprinkle crushed roasted nuts on top after baking.

Place on rack to cool before serving.

**Yam** (*Dioscorea*)
There are many species of yams, some of them dating back to ancient times. The air potato yam is one of the few true yams cultivated for food in the United States. Yams have thick tubers, generally a development at the base of the stem, from which protrude long, slender annual climbing stems, varying in color from white to yellowish-orange.

The thick roots of yams are a major food crop in many tropical countries. They contain mostly water. Much of the solid matter is starch and sugar. The root has less starch than the white potato, but more sugar. Some kind of yams are not fit to eat, but they produce substances called sapogenins that can be used to make drugs such as cortisone.

In many West African countries, the consumption of yams is so great that it is regarded as a staple food. About 20 million tons of yams are grown for food each year. Half of them are grown in the countries of West Africa.

Yams are also grown in India, South-east Asia and the Caribbean.

**Alternate method**

Purée parsnips. Set aside. Purée cooked bulgur. Spread one layer of bulgur, then grated apple and cover with parsnip purée. Sprinkle on Crumb Topping (p. 66) and bake 10–15 minutes or until firm.

Place on a rack to cool before serving.

**Variations**
1. Substitute 1 cup carrot purée for parsnips (p. 63).
2. Substitute 1 cup half-and-half squash-carrot purée for parsnips.
3. Substitute 1/2 cup carrot purée for 1/2 cup parsnip purée.
4. Substitute 1 cup couscous for bulgur (p. 18).
5. Top with fruit purée before baking (p. 64).
6. To make pie more firm, add 2 Tbsp. roasted pastry or chestnut flour to parsnip-bulgur mixture after blending.
7. Adjust liquid content accordingly.

## Candied Yam Pie

Soul food developed out of the slaves' necessity to keep alive on the meager fare allowed them by plantation owners. They lived mainly on vegetables, and used much skill and ingenuity to turn them into the tastiest dishes possible. This is probably how they developed such delicacies as Candied Yam Pie.

1/2 recipe Easy Double Crust Dough (p. 88) or Pressed Pastry (p. 92)

YAM FILLING:
Apple juice to cover yams
8–10 yams (6–7 cups chopped)
1–2 cups chopped carrots
2 Tbsp. oil
3–4 Tbsp. concentrated sweetener
1/2 tsp. salt
1 tsp. cinnamon

1/2 tsp. ginger
1–2 cups Almond Milk (p. 159)
1 tsp. vanilla
3 Tbsp. kuzu or arrowroot flour
TOPPING:
1/2 cup unroasted macadamia nuts

Bring apple juice to a boil. Drop in yams, turn off heat and let sit for a few minutes. Drain, then rinse under cold water immediately. Peel yams and chop. (Save skin for bread or soup if organic.)

Heat oil. Sauté chopped carrots for a few minutes. Add yams, sweetener, salt and spices. Add liquid to almost cover vegetables.

Cover pan and simmer until soft.

After cooking, drain liquid from vegetables. Reserve vegetable juice.

Prepare pie crust. Oil an 8 or 9-inch pie pan. Preheat oven to 375°F.

Prebake pastry 10 minutes.

Blend or purée half to three quarters of the yam mixture. Stir in vanilla.

Combine arrowroot with 2 Tbsp. of cool reserved juice. Mix until creamy and smooth. Stir this mixture into purée and cook until thickened. Combine with unpuréed vegetables.

Fill pie crust with yam mixture and sprinkle crushed macadamias on top. Return to the oven and bake 15–20 minutes longer at 325°F, or until crust is browned and filling is set. Remove and dry. Cool and serve.

### Alternate Method
Brush yams with shoyu and oil. Cover and bake in a 350°F oven until soft. Remove skin. Proceed as in recipe.

## Chestnut-apple Pie

1-1/2 cups dried chestnuts
Apple juice or cider
1 Pressed Pastry (p. 92)

8 cups sliced apples
2 Tbsp. oil
1/2 tsp. sea salt
1 tsp. sea salt
2 tsp. orange rind
3 Tbsp. roasted corn flour

Soak chestnuts in juice or cider to cover overnight. Bring to a boil in water to cover. Cover pot, and cook on a low flame until tender (about 1 hour).

Preheat oven to 375°F. Prebake shell for 15 minutes.

Peel, core and slice apples. Heat oil in a heavy skillet. Add apples and sauté for 5 minutes on a low heat. Add salt, cover and cook until soft.

Combine chestnuts and apples. Add orange rind and flour.

Purée half of chestnut-apple mixture until creamy. Combine purée and other half of mixture. Pour into pie shell.

Bake at 350°F for 10–15 minutes.

## Chiffon Pie

1/2 bar agar-agar
2 cups apple juice
2 egg yolks
1 cup Cashew Milk (p. 159)
2 Tbsp. concentrated sweetener
1 recipe Easy Double Crust Dough
   (p. 88)

Prebake pie shell.

Rinse agar-agar under cold running water.

Squeeze out excess liquid. Shred agar-agar into juice. Bring to a boil. Lower heat and cook until agar-agar is dissolved.

Combine Cashew Milk, concentrated sweetener and cooked agar-agar.

Take a few tsp. of mixture, stir in egg yolks and return yolk combination to mixture. Cook until thickened, stirring continuously. *Do not boil.* Remove from heat, pour into crust and cool.

## Christmas Mincemeat Pie

PRESSED PASTRY:
>     1 cup rolled oats
>     1/2 cup whole wheat pastry flour
>     1/4 tsp. sea salt
>     1/4 cup roasted sesame seeds
>     1/3 cup oil
>     1 Tbsp. concentrated sweetener (enough
>         apple juice or cider to bind crust)

MINCEMEAT FILLING:
>     1 cup raisins
>     Apple juice or cider to soak raisins
>     1 cup Apricot Purée (p. 64)
>     2 cups diced apples
>     Juice and rind of 1/2 lemon
>     Juice and rind of 1/2 orange
>     1 tsp. cinnamon
>     1/4 tsp. cloves
>     1/4 tsp. ginger
>     1-1/2 Tbsp. miso

*Pressed pastry*

Combine oats and pastry flour in a mixing bowl. Add sea salt and sesame seeds. Rub oil in slowly until it resembles bread crumbs. Put a handful of mixture in the palm of your hand, make a fist and open hand. If the mixture almost sticks together, then the amount of oil is sufficient.

Moisten with concentrated sweetener until it binds together. Press into oiled pan. (Do not add too much liquid or the crust will not be flaky.)

Preheat oven to 375°F. Bake crust 10 minutes.

*Mincemeat Filling*

Soak raisins in apple juice or cider to cover until soft. Reserve liquid. Prepare Apricot Purée. Reserve excess liquid.

Core and dice apples. (Peel if not organic.) Combine juice and rinds of lemon and orange, and spices with the Apricot Purée. Combine the miso and apricot-purée mixture. Fold in the diced apples and raisins.

Place Mincement Filling in the pastry shell and bake 10 minutes longer or until firm.

## Melon Cream Pie

>     1 recipe Pressed Pastry

FILLING:
>     4 cups diced melon (Cantaloupe is good
>         for this)
>     2 Tbsp. oil
>     1/4 tsp. sea salt
>     3 Tbsp. tahini
>     4 cups apple juice or cider
>     1 bar agar-agar
>     1–2 tsp. cinnamon
>     1/2–1 tsp. ginger
>     4 Tbsp. arrowroot flour

TOPPING:
>     Tofu Cream (p. 147)
>     Strawberries for garnish

Prebake pie shell. Set aside to cool.

Remove skin and seeds, and dice melon. Sauté melon in oil over a medium heat for 5 minutes. Add salt and simmer uncovered about 5 minutes longer.

Blend tahini, half of melon mixture, and 1 cup apple juice or cider together, until creamy and smooth.

Rinse agar-agar under cold running water. Squeeze out excess liquid. Shred into small pieces. Combine with 2 cups apple juice or cider, and cook on a medium heat until mixture begins to boil. Lower heat and simmer until agar-agar dissolves. Add blended melon-tahini mixture and spices to agar-agar. Bring to boil.

Dilute arrowroot in 1 cup apple juice or cider, and stir into mixture rapidly until it boils again and begins to thicken. Remove from heat and set aside to cool.* Prepare Tofu Cream. Set aside.

---

* Pie shells have a tendency to crack if they have not cooled completely before being filled, or if filling is at a different temperature from crust.

Pour cool melon mixture into shell before it jells. Set aside to harden at room temperature. (You may chill at this time, but it is advisable to wait until it is completely cool.)

Spoon Tofu Cream over the top of the pie after the pie has set. Garnish with strawberries. Chill before serving.

## Lemon Meringue Pie

 1 recipe Pressed Pastry (p. 92)
FILLING:
 1 bar agar-agar
 4 cups apple juice or cider
 Pinch of sea salt
 1 Tbsp. concentrated sweetener
 6 Tbsp. arrowroot flour
 Juice of 1-1/2 lemons or grated rind
  and juice of 1/2 lemon
 1 tsp. vanilla
MERINGUE:
 2–3 Tbsp. concentrated sweetener
 2 egg whites
 Pinch of sea salt
 1/2 tsp. vanilla
 1 tsp. lemon, orange rind or mint

Prepare pastry.

Preheat oven to 375°F. Bake crust 15 minutes or until lightly browned (not quite completely baked).

*Filling*

Wash agar-agar under cold running water. Squeeze out liquid and shred into apple juice (reserve 1/2 cup apple juice for arrowroot). Add salt.

Cook on a medium heat until mixture boils; reduce heat and simmer until agar-agar dissolves.

Dilute arrowroot in 1/2 cup apple juice and sweetener.

Add arrowroot to agar-agar, and cook on a high heat, stirring constantly, until the mixture boils, starts to thicken and turns clear. Stir in lemon juice and vanilla, remove

from heat and let set 5 minutes.

Pour lemon-agar-agar filling into shell. Allow to cool.

*Meringue*

Cook sweetener in a heavy saucepan or double boiler until it reaches a temperature of 265°F (use a candy thermometer).

Beat egg whites and sea salt together. Slowly drip the sweetener into the whites, while beating. Beat until stiff. Add vanilla and other flavoring, and beat until peaked.

Spread on top of dessert. Bake at 225°F for 45 minutes, at 325°F for 25 minutes or at 400°F for 10 minutes.

Turn off oven, open door, and leave inside at least 15 minutes longer.

## Orange Cream Pie

NUT PIE CRUST:
 1-1/2 cups sifted whole wheat pastry
  flour
 1 tsp. cinnamon or mint
 1/4 tsp. sea salt
 1/4 cup ground roasted nuts or seeds
 1/4 cup oil
 1/2–1 cup apple juice, cider, mu tea, or
  mint tea
ORANGE CREAM:
 1 bar agar-agar
 1/2 cup apple juice or cider
 2-1/2 cups Oat Cream (p. 145)
 1 egg
 2 Tbsp. concentrated sweetener
 1 tsp. vanilla
 Juice and rind of 1/2 grated orange
 1/2 tsp. cinnamon
 1/4 tsp. sea salt

*Nut pie crust*

Sift the flour into a mixing bowl. Combine all dry ingredients. Cut the oil through the dry mixture until it looks like fine bread crumbs. *Do not knead or overwork the flour.* Too much movement activates the gluten, resulting in a hard crust.

Add enough liquid to form a soft dough. Roll out pastry. Place in oiled pie dish and bake in preheated 375°F oven 15–20 minutes.

*Filling*

Rinse agar-agar under cold running watter. Squeeze out excess liquid. Shred into 1/2 cup apple juice, bring to a boil and cook on a medium heat until agar-agar dissolves. Add Oat Cream, lower heat and simmer 5 minutes longer.

Separate egg. Combine yolk, sweetener, vanilla, orange juice and grated rind. Beat until fluffy. Combine with Oat Cream mixture and blend until smooth and creamy, adding cinnamon gradually.

Beat egg white and sea salt together until peaked. Fold egg white into cream gently. Place entire mixture into half-baked crust and bake until set.

You may substitute lemon juice and rind for orange juice and rind.

## Pear and Ginger Crisp

> 1/2 cup raisins
> 2–3 cups Almond Milk (p. 159) or cider
> 14 cups sliced pears
> 1 tsp. ginger powder
> 1/2 cup corn flour or sweet brown rice flour
> 1/2 tsp. sea salt
> 1 tsp. cinnamon
> 1 tsp. vanilla
> 1-1/2 cups Crumb Topping (p. 66)

Soak raisins in sweet Almond Milk or cider to cover until soft. Drain. Set raisins aside.

Core and slice pears (peel if not organic).

Roast the flour in a dry skillet until it begins to smell sweet and is lightly browned. Set aside to cool. Preheat oven to 350°F.

Combine the roasted flour and Almond Milk. Add cinnamon, ginger, and salt. Add pears, raisins and vanilla, and mix gently until the fruit is coated with the liquid mixture. Place in baking dish, cover and bake 30 minutes. Remove cover, sprinkle on Crumb Topping and bake until browned.

**Variations**

Add 1 Tbsp. orange rind.

Dilute 2 Tbsp. tahini or almond butter in apple juice before adding it to flour combination.

Substitute any fresh fruit in season for pears.

**Pear** (*Pyrus communis*)

There are many different varieties of pears found all over the world. They resemble the apple in many ways, but have a more elongated fruit. The tree grows wild in most parts of Europe, but more in the warmer southern parts than in the north. Many different kinds of pears are cultivated today, varying from round to top-shaped to oval shape, and red, brown, green, yellow or golden russet in color.

The fruits may be eaten raw, stewed, cooked like applesauce, or used in dessert making for pastries, pies or cakes.

## Pear Cream Pie

> 1 Nut Pie Crust (p. 93)
> 2 cups Tofu Cream (p. 147)
> 1 bar agar-agar
> 2 cups apple juice or cider
> 4 cups sliced pears
> Vanilla
> Crushed roasted nuts

Prebake pie shel. Prepare Tofu Cream.

Rinse agar-agar, shred into apple juice and bring to a boil. Lower heat and simmer until the agar-agar dissolves.

Add half of the pears and vanilla to agar-agar mixture. Stir well.

Fold half of cream into agar-agar mixture. Cook on a low heat for 3 minutes, stirring constantly. Spoon mixture into prebaked shell.

Chill until almost firm, then add remaining pears to remaining cream, and spread over top.

Garnish with crushed roasted nuts. Chill until firm.

## Poppy-seed-apricot Layer Pie

> 1 recipe Pressed Pastry (p. 92)
> 2 cups Apricot Purée (p. 64)
> 3 Tbsp. arrowroot flour
> 2 cups Poppy Seed Filling (p. 88)

Prebake pie shell at 375°F for 15–20 minutes, or until golden brown.

Combine apricot purée with 3 Tbsp. sifted arrowroot flour. Cook, stirring constantly, until mixture begins to boil.

Pour into prebaked shell. (The shell should be the same temperature as the filling.)

Top with Poppy Seed Filling. (This mixture should contain almost no liquid.) Allow to set. Chill before serving.

## Spinach Pie

> PHYLLO PASTRY:
> 2 cups whole wheat pastry flour
> 1/2 tsp. sea salt
> 2/3 cups warm water
> 1/4 cup olive oil
> FILLING:
> 1 lb. spinach
> 3 cups pressed and mashed tofu
> 2 cups diced onion
> 4 Tbsp. olive oil
> 1 tsp. dill seed (crush for more flavor)
> Sea salt
> 2–3 Tbsp. miso creamed in small amount of warm water
> 3 beaten eggs

*Phyllo pastry*

Combine flour and salt together. Heat water until warm. Combine with oil and beat together until cloudy.

Make a well in the center of the flour. Pour the liquid and oil in all at once and mix until the dough comes away from the sides of the bowl.

Knead 10 minutes. After shaping into round ball, cover the dough with oil. Place cloth on top and set at room temperature at least 1 hour.

*Filling*

Drop spinach into boiling salted water and bring to a boil. Drain off liquid and discard. Rinse spinach under cold water and squeeze out liquid. Set aside.

Heat skillet and dry roast tofu without oil, sprinkling in sea salt as you roast to help evaporate water more quickly. Move tofu continuously until dry and cheese-like. Set aside.

Dice onion. Heat skillet; add oil and sauté onion on a medium heat until lightly browned. Mix in the spinach and tofu. Cook 5 minutes. Sprinkle in crushed dill seed, mix and remove from heat.

Cream in miso and stir until well combined with spinach-tofu mixture. Cool. When mixture is room temperature, stir in beaten eggs.

*Rolling out pastry dough*

Roll out pastry into log. Divide into five pieces, covering four with cloth until ready to use.

Shape pastry into rectangle.

Oil rectangular pan (about 10 × 12 inches). Preheat oven to 400°F.

Sprinkle arrowroot flour on cloth or

greaseproof paper. Begin to roll out pastry to shape of baking pan. Make the pastry slightly larger than the size of the pan.

Roll the pastry around rolling pin making sure that the pastry is well floured. (This helps to make sure that the pastry does not stick to itself or the rolling pin.)

Unroll into baking pan. Trim off excess so that pastry just fits into the bottom of the pan (no sides).

Brush pastry with a lot of oil.

Repeat with one more layer, brushing with oil.

Spread on filling and cover with three more layers of pastry, brushing with oil in between each layer. Score.

Brush top layer with oil. Sprinkle cold water on top.

Bake 40–50 minutes or until lightly browned. Serve while still warm.

## Sunshine Pie (Savory)

> 1 recipe Pressed Pastry (p. 92)
> 4 cups yam or sweet potato purée
>   (p. 63)
> 2 Tbsp. arrowroot flour or kuzu
> 4 Tbsp. sesame butter
> 1 tsp. ginger
> 1/2 tsp. cinnamon
> 1/2 tsp. sea salt or 1 Tbsp. miso
> 1/4 cup concentrated sweetener
>   (optional)
> 1/2 cup unroasted crushed pecans
> Roasted pecan halves

Preheat oven to 350°F. Prepare crust and prebake 10 minutes.

Combine purée, arrowroot flour, sesame butter, ginger, cinnamon, salt and sweetener in a saucepan. Cook, stirring constantly, until thickened. Fill shell with mixture and bake 20–25 minutes, or until crust is golden brown.

Sprinkle crushed pecans on top of pie 10 minutes before removing from oven.

Place the pecan halves on top for decoration after baking.

## Tarts

A tart is a delicate, small pie, made from deep-fried or baked pastry. It can be filled with cooked or raw fruit, vegetables, custards, creams, jellies or a combination of these.

Any pie filling can be used for tarts, and vice versa. Tarts can be kept for several weeks before filling.

*Lining Tart Forms*

Place 12 tart forms touching one another in rows of four. Roll out pastry 1/4 inch thick to a size 3–4 inches larger than the area covered by the forms.

1. Fold the dough back twice, until you have a long, narrow piece of dough, which you can lift and place on top of the forms.

2. Place dough on forms nearest you, and unfold outward to cover the others. Let pastry stand 10 minutes to settle naturally. It will stretch and fall into forms.

3. Cover pastry-lined forms with a towel or canvas cloth, and run a rolling pin over the top of the forms.

4. Form a small ball the size of a walnut from the leftover scraps of pastry dough. Use this to press pastry firmly into forms.

Cover and chill 30 minutes before baking.

*Praparation*

*Unfilled tarts*

To bake unfilled tarts, place them on a baking sheet and bake 10–15 minutes at 375°F. Then fill three-quarters full and bake 15 minutes longer, or until they begin to bubble (with fruit filling), or get firm (creams and custards), or get dry (purées).

*Filled tarts*

To bake filled, fill tart three-quarters full and place on a baking sheet. Bake until the fruit fillings begin to rise, and get juicy and bubbly, or until the creams or custards get firm, or until the purées get dry.

## Variations

1. Bake or deep-fry unfilled. Cool. Place 1 Tbsp. cream (p. 144) in each tart. Allow to set for a few minutes. Cover with slices of cooked fruit or vegetables. Brush with apricot glaze (see Fruit Glaze, p. 62) and serve.
2. Line form with pastry, cover and chill 30 minutes. Heat oil. Deep-fry pastry dough and shell together. They will separate in the hot oil. Remove form and continue frying dough until lightly browned, and the oil has almost completely stopped bubbling around the edges of the tart. Drain and cool. Fill with filling the same temperature as the tart (preferably cool).

## Lattice Apple Tart I

1 Easy Double Crust Pastry (p. 88)
1 cup raisins
4 lbs. apples
apple juice

2 Tbsp. oil
Juice and rind of 1 lemon
1 Tbsp. miso
1/2–1 cup apricot glaze (see Fruit Glaze, p. 62)
1 cup Crumb Topping (p. 66)

Prepare pastry. Oil a shallow 9 or 10-inch rectangular sheet or 12 tart forms. Line the sheet or forms with pastry. Save the extra dough for the top. Cover and chill sheet at least 30 minutes.

*Filling*

Soak raisins in juice to cover until soft. Drain. Reserve liquid.

Core apples (peel if not organic) and cut into eight.

Heat oil in a heavy skillet or pan. Sauté apples for a few minutes, add lemon juice, rind, and miso. Cover and cook 2 minutes; remove cover and cook until slightly tender. Add raisins and cool.

Preheat oven to 375°F. Prebake pastry 10 minutes. Fill with apple mixture.

*Lattice top*

Roll out a strip of dough 1/8 inch thick. Brush with oil, and sprinkle with Crumb Topping to make it adhere better.

Cut into strips 1/4 inch wide. (To cut strips, use a pastry wheel to give a fluted edge.)

Lattice the pastry strips on top of the apple filling.

Bake in 350°F oven for 30 minutes or until filling begins to bubble in the center. The last 10 minutes of baking time, place the tarts on a higher rack in the oven to brown the lattice top.

Prepare apricot glaze. Remove tarts from oven, and place on rack to cool.

While still warm, brush with hot apricot glaze.

## Apple Tart II

Follow directions for Apple Tart I. Soak apples in the juice of 1 lemon and 1 tsp. vanilla. Drain off liquid. (Use for glazes, fillings, cake liquid.) Sauté half of the apple mixture until soft. Place in tart shells.

Arrange the remaining apples overlapping each other on top of apple filling.

Bake in 350°F oven for 30 minutes. Sprinkle chopped nuts on top of tarts the last 10 minutes of baking time.

Remove from oven and cool on rack before removing from forms.

## Carrot Tart

    8–10 medium-size carrots
    2 Tbsp. oil
    1 tsp. grated ginger
    1/2 tsp. sea salt
    1/4 cup apple juice or cider
    3 Tbsp. chestnut or whole wheat pastry
      flour
    1 Pressed Pastry (p. 92)
    1/2 cup Nut Filling (p. 65)
    1 cup roasted, crushed nuts

Dice carrots. Sauté in oil. Add ginger, salt and apple juice. Cover and cook until tender. Purée.

Roast flour. Set aside to cool. Preheat oven to 375°F.

Prepare pastry. Roll out dough and place in oiled forms. Sprinkle Nut Filling and nuts in tarts.

Cut strips for lattice top.

Combine cooled roasted flour with carrot purée.

Prebake tarts 10 minutes. Spoon filling into them. Bake 15–20 minutes.

**Cherry** (*Prunus cerasus*)
There are many different varieties of cherries, ranging from sour to sweet. Cultivated cherries are either dark red-black or pale yellow, covered with a red hue. There are beautiful white or pinkish flowers which are produced in clusters, bearing forth shiny fruit on long flower stalks. The cherry tree grows up to 75 feet in height in well-drained woodlands. Used as a fresh fruit dessert in the summertime, the cherry is also traditionally used for cherry pie, tarts and custard.

## Tofu Sour Cream Cheese Tart

This tart can also be made with peaches, apricots, pears or any fresh fruit in season.

    1 recipe Phyllo Pastry (p. 95)
    3 cups pitted cherries
    2 eggs
    1 cup Tofu Sour Cream (p. 147)
    3 Tbsp. concentrated sweetener
    1/2 tsp. vanilla

Prepare pastry. Oil a 9 or 10-inch pan (about 1 inch deep), or 9–12 tart forms. Line with pastry (p. 96). Cover and chill 30 minutes.

Wash and pit cherries. Cut into small pieces. If using other fruit, slice, and peel if not organic.

Preheat oven to 375°F. Prebake pastry 10 minutes.

Beat eggs with Tofu Sour Cream, sweetener and vanilla. Arrange fruit in tarts. Pour egg mixture over fruit, and bake on lowest rack in oven for 15 minutes, or until custard is firm.

### Variations

Substitute any fresh or dried fruit for cherries.

Substitute any cream for Tofu Sour Cream.

## Walnut Tart

> 1 recipe Pressed Pastry (p. 92)
> 1 cup unroasted walnuts
> 1 tsp. cinnamon
> 1 cup Fruit Purée (p. 64)
> 3 eggs
> 1 tsp. vanilla
> 1/2 tsp. sea salt
> 1/4 cup concentrated sweetener
> 1/4 cup whole wheat pastry flour
> 1/4 cup arrowroot flour

Prepare pastry. Oil a 9 or 10-inch tart pan (1 inch deep) or tart forms. Line with pastry, cover and chill at least 30 minutes.

Preheat oven to 375°F.

Roast the walnuts; while they are warm, grind finely. Mix with cinnamon, and press into the bottom of the chilled pastry.

Prebake 10 minutes. Spread Fruit Purée on top of pastry.

Separate eggs. Set whites aside. Stir yolks lightly to break them up. Add vanilla and set aside.

Beat egg whites and salt until foamy. Slowly begin to drip in sweetener, beating continuously. Fold one quarter of whites into yolks. Sift flours.

Combine yolk mixture and whites, and slowly fold together, sprinkling flour in as you fold. *Do not overmix.* Place on top of

fruit purée. Bake 10–15 minutes, or until lightly browned.

## Strudels

### Apple Walnut Strudel

FILLING:
> 1 cup raisin or sultanas
> Apple juice or cider
> 2 cups chopped apples
> 2–3 cups chopped roasted walnuts
> 1 Tbsp. cinnamon

STRUDEL PASTRY:
> 2 cups whole wheat pastry flour or
>   1 cup whole wheat pastry flour and
>   1 cup sifted whole wheat flour
> 1/2 tsp. sea salt
> 1/4 cup oil
> 1 Tbsp. orange or lemon juice
> 2 egg whites
> 2/3–1 cup lukewarm apple juice, cider
>   or raisin juice
> Arrowroot flour
> 3–4 Tbsp. tahini or almond butter

*Filling*

Soak raisins or sultanas in apple juice or cider to cover until soft. (Drain off liquid and use for dough.) Core and chop apples, and mix with sultanas, walnuts and cinnamon. Set aside.

*Strudel pastry*

Place flour and sea salt in a mixing bowl. Cut in oil. Add orange or lemon juice, and egg whites. Pour in apple juice gradually until a very soft, sticky dough is formed.

Knead on a floured surface until smooth and elastic. Place in an oiled bowl, brush the top of the dough with oil. Cover and set in a warm place. If there is no warm spot, place bowl in a pan of hot water until dough becomes lukewarm.

*Filling the strudel*

Preheat oven to 375°F. Oil baking sheets.

Cover surface of dough with a pastry cloth or greaseproof paper. Sprinkle arrowroot onto surface. Roll out dough in rectangular shape until 1/8 inch thick. Brush entire surface with oil. Allow dough to rest 5–10 minutes. Trim edges.

Spread surface of dough with tahini, leaving a 2-inch border on two ends. Sprinkle some apple-walnut filling over surface.

Fold over edges that do not have any filling on them toward the center. Brush with oil.

Lift up the edge of the pastry cloth nearest you and begin to flip the dough over on the filling.

Continue until the dough is completely rolled around itself. Flip the dough onto a well-oiled baking sheet. Slit the top and bake, glazing before or after baking.

## Chestnut Orange Strudel

> Any yeasted or unyeasted dough
> 1–2 cups Chestnut Cream (p. 144)
> 1–2 tsp. orange rind
> 1/2 tsp. rose water
> Egg yolk

Roll out dough on cloth or greaseproof paper.

Combine orange rind with Chestnut Cream and rose water.

Place a 3-inch strip of filling across the bottom end of strudel.

Fold in the end of the pastry on both sides.

Brush with oil.

Lift up the end of the cloth nearest the filling, and fold the dough over onto the filling.

Raise the pastry cloth or greaseproof paper and continue until the dough is completely rolled.

Flip the dough onto a well-oiled baking sheet. Slit top, glaze with egg yolk. Bake in preheated 375°F oven 30–40 minutes.

**Variation**

*Fruit-filled slit strudel:* Prepare yeasted dough (p. 104). Roll into rectangle 1/2 inch thick. Place filling in the center third of dough. Slit both sides of unfilled dough diagonally 1/2 inch apart, from filling to edge.

Fold strips alternately over filling, stretching and twisting slightly. Allow to rise. Bake in a preheated 375°F oven 30–40 minutes.

## Cherry Tofu Strudel

Substitute 4 cups pitted fresh chopped cherries and 2 cups Tofu Sour Cream (p. 147) for apple-walnut filling. Combine tofu and cherries. Fill.

## Mincemeat Strudel

Substitute Mincemeat Filling (p. 92) for apple-walnut filling.

## Cinnamon-nut Strudel

> 1 cup chopped walnuts

1/2 cup blanched chopped almonds
1 tsp. cinnamon
2 recipes Hot Water Pastry Dough
   (p. 84)
1 cup olive oil

CINNAMON SYRUP:
1/4 cup concentrated sweetener
1 cinnamon stick or 1 tsp. cinnamon
1 tsp. lemon juice

Combine walnuts, almonds and cinnamon. Set aside. Prepare dough. Roll into thin sheets.

Brush half of a 7×12-inch pastry sheet with oil. Fold over the other half, and brush with more oil. Sprinkle with 1 Tbsp. nut mixture.

Roll dough up like a strudel, very tightly. Cut strudel in half, making two rolls.

*Cinnamon syrup*

Combine sweetener and cinnamon stick or cinnamon. Cook 10 minutes over a low flame. Add lemon juice and remove from heat.

Preheat oven to 350°F. Oil a baking sheet lightly. Place strudel on baking sheet. Slit top. Bake 25–30 minutes, or until browned. Place on a rack with a pan underneath to catch drippings, and pour warm cinnamon syrup over pastry.

# 6. HIGHER AND HIGHER: Yeasted Pastries

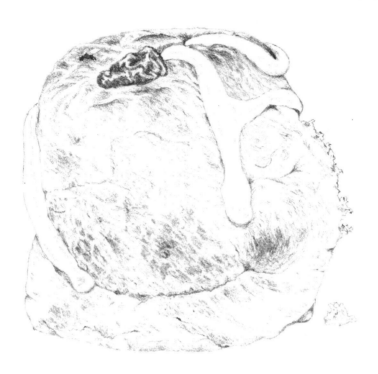

The fine art of baking was first enhanced by the use of yeast in Egypt around 4000 B.C. Yeast is a living bacteria which feeds on natural sugar from grain, as well as from added sugar. The natural, simple sugars in flour are usually not enough to let the yeast work quickly, so sugar obtained from cane, honey, syrups and various fruits and juices are added. This allows the yeast to change the oxygen and sugar in flour into carbon dioxide and alcohol more rapidly.

Beating or kneading the batter or dough activates the gluten, causing the alcohol to evaporate and the carbon dioxide to become caught in the gluten, making the dough rise. During baking, the high oven temperature drives off the alcohol and expands the gas bubbles, enlarging the little holes in the dough and causing it to rise even more.

There is a lifelike quality to yeasted doughs which can only be felt during the transformation of a doughy mass into a finely sculptured pastry or cake. Braiding, twisting, swirling are only a few of the many ways in which you can have fun working with yeasted dough.

# Working with Yeast

There are many ways to prepare yeasted doughs or batters for pastries and cakes. The recipes in this section usually begin by first preparing a "sponge," or first-rise batter. The advantage of this method is that the yeast will get started more quickly and easily in the absence of the other ingredients, especially salt, which can delay or inhibit the yeasted batter or dough's rising action. However, if you are pressed for time, the first-rise batter may be omitted.

### Sponge Preparation

Dilute the yeast (dry or cake) with a small amount (1/2 cup) of lukewarm (75° to 90°F) apple juice or cider.* Stir until all the lumps have dissolved, and set aside for about 5 minutes, or until it begins to bubble. Add enough whole wheat flour or whole wheat pastry flour to yeasted mixture to form a thin batter. Beat for several minutes with a wooden spoon or wire whisk. Cover with a damp cloth and set in a warm place to rise until it is doubled in size. Beat down, add the rest of the ingredients and follow the recipe.

### Kneading

Kneading does not refer only to bread-making. This process develops the gluten in flour, allowing the dough to rise, and forming lighter, moister cakes or pastries. This kneading technique is used when the yeasted mixture is too thick to be beaten with a wooden spoon. If your dough is soft and sticky to the touch, you can knead it directly in the mixing bowl.

### Kneading soft dough in a bowl
Flour your hands. Pull the soft dough over and over from the side of the bowl to the center, holding the bowl steady as you pull. Knead dough until it begins to pull away from the side of the bowl (10 to 15 minutes).

### Kneading heavier dough on a flat surface
Flour your hands if the dough is sticky.

Knead dough on a pastry cloth or wooden board lightly dusted with flour. Using the heels of your hands, press down firmly, folding the dough in half. Press down again with the heels of your hands, rotating it slightly. Repeat over and over again until the dough feels smooth and elastic. Do not be afraid to press firmly and punch the dough, because it is this movement that will activate the gluten in the flour and make the dough rise. When the dough is smooth, place it in a large oiled bowl; oil the top of the dough to prevent it from drying out. Cover and place in a warm spot, let rise until doubled in size.

---

* These liquids, which contain natural sugar, help the yeast to work quickly.

# Forget Me Knots

1. Rising times will vary according to the temperature and moisture of the room, the flour, the ingredients in the dough or batter, the shape of the dough and the general weather of the day.

2. The amount of liquid necessary for each dough or batter will vary according to the temperature and moisture of the room, the flour and the general weather of the day.

3. *Compressed Yeast:* Compressed yeast cakes contain live active yeast plants. Use lukewarm liquid to dissolve compressed yeast. A drop of liquid which feels comfortable when placed on the inside of the wrist is lukewarm.

4. *Dry Yeast:* Dry yeast is prepared by mixing the plant with starch, pressing the mixture and then drying it at a low heat. In order to grow again, the yeast must be dissolved in warm liquid and some kind of sugar (such as apple juice).

   Dry yeast, unlike fresh yeast, may be kept refrigerated in a well-sealed container for many months without losing its rising powers. It cannot decay or mold since it contains no moisture.

   Use slightly warmer liquid (90° to 100°F) to dissolve active dry yeast. Place your finger in the liquid; if you are able to keep your finger there without discomfort it is the right temperature.

5. A temperature of 145°F will make the yeast inactive.

6. Fill pans, forms or sheets only halfway, to allow batter or dough to rise.

7. Always slit the top of a yeasted pastry before it rises, to allow for greater expansion.

8. When covering the pan containing the yeasted batter or dough for the final rise, use a glass pan as cover. This will enable you to see the rate of expansion so that the dough does not over-rise.

9. Oil the rim of the pan used for covering dough or batter, so that the dough or batter does not stick to it when rising.

10. To test dough for rising: A slight impression will remain when you press the dough lightly with your fingers. To test batters for rising, touch the batter lightly with finger. If sufficiently risen, the batter should stick to your finger, and air holes should be visible when finger is removed.

11. If the dough or batter has over-risen, it will fall while baking. In this event, it is best to prepare the dough or batter all over again because the yeast has probably died (become inactive).

12. To retard rising, place the dough or batter in an oiled pan or bowl, oil the surface of the dough, cover with a damp cloth and chill until ready to use.

13. The consistency of yeasted batters should be that of thick pancake batter dropping with difficulty from a wooden spoon.

14. Glaze yeasted dough before rising, or before, during or after baking (p. 82). If using an egg glaze, it is best to glaze immediately before or during baking to avoid slowing down the rising process.

15. Add dried fruit, crushed nuts, seeds or extra spices to dough after the first rise.

16. Shape dough into desired form before rolling out.

17. Ready or not: Tap pastry lightly on the

bottom. There will be a hollow sound when done. Pastry will be firm but not hard.

18. The sweeter the dough, the more oil it will absorb when deep-frying.

19. Try interchanging unyeasted and yeasted pastry doughs (see chapter 5).

20. To preserve yeasted cakes or pastries, place a small, damp paper napkin with the yeasted products. Keep container tightly sealed and in a cool place.

# Recipes

## All Around Yeasted Pastry

    1 Tbsp. dry yeast
    3/4–1-1/2 cups apple juice or cider
    2–4 Tbsp. concentrated sweetener
    2 beaten eggs
    3 cups whole wheat pastry flour
    1/2 cup oil
    1/2 tsp. sea salt
    1 tsp. vanilla
    2 tsp. cinnamon
    1 Tbsp. orange and lemon rind

Dissolve yeast in 1/2 cup lukewarm apple juice or cider, add sweetener. Stir and set aside 5 minutes or until mixture bubbles. Add eggs and enough flour to form a thin batter. Beat until smooth and not lumpy. Clean down the sides of the bowl with a rubber spatula. Cover and let rise in a warm spot until it is almost doubled in size. Beat in oil, salt and vanilla. Combine the rest of the dry ingredients, reserving 1/2 cup of flour, and beat into yeasted mixture until it is too hard to beat. Add only enough apple juice or cider to form a soft sticky dough.

Knead dough on a lightly floured surface, kneading in the reserved flour if necessary to make the dough perfectly smooth. Place in an oiled bowl, cover and let rise in a warm spot until doubled in size. (After rising, it should feel soft and puffy).

Roll and shape the dough into desired form. Place it on an oiled baking tray, cover with another tray to allow room for expansion. Let rise until almost double in size. Punch down, shape and bake.

**Blueberry** (*Ericaceae*)
Blueberries grow wild in many parts of the world. However, the U.S. and Canada supply about 95 percent of the blueberries used by the food industry.

The food industry uses two main kinds of blueberries, lowbush and highbush. Lowbush blueberry shrubs grow wild and measure about 6 to 18 inches tall. Farmers generally gather the wild berries and sell them for processed foods.

The highbush berries, make up most of the fresh blueberries sold in groceries. Ripe blueberries range in color from light blue to black and have a waxy, powdery-gray coating. They have green leaves and white or pink flowers.

## Fruit Pizza

There are many ways to make a sweet pizza. Each province in Italy has its own specialty. This pizza has been adapted from the Sicilian "fruit pizza."

1 recipe Yeasted Pastry (p. 106)
2 Tbsp. orange juice
1 Tbsp. orange rind
FILLING:
    4 medium-size apples
    2 cups Apricot Purée (p. 64)
TOPPING:
    Crumb Topping (p. 66)

Oil an 8-inch round pizza tray. Prepare dough. Roll out to 1/4-inch thickness and place on the bottom of the tray. Cover and let rise.

Core and cut apples into 1/2-inch slices. (Peel if not organic.)

Preheat oven to 350°F. Prebake crust 10 minutes. Spread purée over dough, and place apples on top. Sprinkle Crumb. Topping over filling. Bake 15 minutes longer, or until apples are tender and dough is lightly browned.

## Blueberry Peach Pizza

1 recipe Yeasted Pastry (p. 106)
2 Tbsp. orange juice
1 Tbsp. orange rind
FILLING:
    5 medium-size peaches
    3 cups blueberries
    1 tsp. ginger
    1 tsp. lemon juice
    1 Tbsp. tahini
TOPPING:
    Crumb Topping (p. 66)
    1/2 cup unsweetened coconut (optional)

Blanch peaches (p. 16); slice into 1/4-inch pieces. Prepare dough. Combine peaches, blueberries, ginger, lemon juice and tahini in a mixing bowl. Toss lightly until fruit is coated. Set aside for 15 minutes. Prepare topping. (Add coconut if desired.) Set aside.

Preheat oven to 350°F. Oil a round 8-inch pizza tray. Follow Fruit-Pizza method.

## Cherry Balls

1 recipe Yeasted Pastry Dough (p. 106)
2 cups cherries
1/2 cup apple juice or cider
2 tsp. vanilla
Chopped roasted pine nuts

Shape dough into balls, and place them in an oiled pan 1 inch apart. Cover and set in warm place to rise until almost doubled in size. Chop cherries. Combine cherries, juice and vanilla. Spoon on top of and in between the balls.

Preheat oven to 375°F. Bake 20 minutes covered; remove cover and bake 20 to 30 minutes longer, or until browned. Remove from oven and cool.

Sprinkle nuts over top just before serving.

## Bowknots

Yeasted Pastry Dough (p. 106)
Oil for deep-frying (p. 16)
Roasted chestunut flour for dusting

*Deep-frying for unyeasted or yeasted dough*
Prepare dough. Sprinkle pastry cloth or wooden surface with arrowroot flour. Divide dough into four parts. Roll out one piece of dough into thin log. Cover the rest of the dough with a damp cloth and set aside.

Cut into strips 6 × 1 inches. Tie in Bowknots.

Repeat procedure until all the dough is shaped. (For yeasted dough, cover and let rise until almost double in size.)

Heat oil. Deep-fry until delicately brown. Drain, dust with cinnamon immediately and cool.

*Baking for unyeasted or yeasted dough*

Roll out into desired shape. Place on a baking sheet, cover and let rise in a warm place until almost double in size. (For unyeasted dough, bake immediately after shaping.)

Bake at 350°F for 25–30 minutes, or until lightly browned. Brush with concentrated sweetener immediately after baking.

## Blueberry-peach Turnovers

2–3 cups sliced peaches
2–3 cups blueberries
1 tsp. cinnamon
1 tsp. orange rind plus 1 Tbsp. kuzu
1/4 tsp. sea salt
1 recipe Yeasted Pastry Dough (p. 106)

Slice peaches (Peel if not organic.) and mix with blueberries, cinnamon, orange rind, kuzu and salt. Let sit at least 30 minutes. Prepare dough.

Flour surface, sprinkling cinnamon over flour. Shape dough into square before rolling. Roll out to 1/4-inch thickness. Trim edges. Cut pastry into 4 or 5-inch squares.

Drain excess liquid from fruit mixture. Place a tsp. of filling in the center of each square. Fold over one corner of the square to make a triangle.

Press dough firmly around edges of pastry with the back or front of a fork. Oil a shallow pan or cookie sheet. Place pastries on sheet 2 inches apart. Slit each one diagonally twice to allow steam to escape.

Cover and set in a warm place to rise until almost double in size.

Preheat the oven to 350°F. Glaze before or after baking (p. 82). Bake about 30–40 minutes, or until turnovers are browned.

## Bow Ties

1 recipe Yeasted Pastry Dough (p. 106)
Any Fruit Purée (p. 64) or Nut Butter
    Icing (p. 60)
Nut Filling (p. 65)

Shape dough into rectangle. Roll out dough 1/4 inch thick and cut away uneven edges. Cut into 2 × 5-inch strips. Brush with purée or Nut Butter Icing, and sprinkle over Nut Filling.

Twist each end of the strip from the center in the opposite direction so that a bow is formed and fillings are face up. Place on an oiled baking sheet. Cover and let rise until almost doubled in size.

Preheat the oven to 350°F. Glaze before or after baking (p. 82). Bake 20–30 minutes, or until brown.

### Variation

Cut into strips 2 × 10 inches. Brush with purée or icing and sprinkle filling on top. Fold strips over lengthwise, making them half as long. Slit the centers. Twist each end of strip in the opposite direction until a bow is formed.

# Cinnamon Rolls

> 4–6 cups raisins
> Apple juice
> 1 recipe Yeasted Pastry Dough (p. 106)
> Date purée (p. 64)
> Cinnamon
> TOPPING:
> 1 cup Tofu Sour Cream (p. 147)
> 1/4 cup concentrated sweetener
> 1 tsp. vanilla

Soak raisins in apple juice to cover until soft. Squeeze out excess liquid. Divide the dough in half.

On a *lightly* floured board, cloth or grease-proof paper, roll out half of the dough to a rectangle. Brush with oil. Spread date purée over dough. Sprinkle cinnamon liberally over the date purée. Cover with raisins. Roll up from the side like a jelly roll (see Swiss Roll, p. 45). Cut into 1-inch slices and place cut side up on an oiled baking sheet, or in muffin tins.

Repeat procedure with other half of the dough. Cover and let rise in a warm place until almost doubled in size.

Preheat oven to 350°F. Bake 15 minutes.

Combine Tofu Sour Cream with sweetener and vanilla. Spoon over the rolls. Bake 10–15 minutes longer.

# Crumb Swirl

Prepare Yeasted Pastry Dough (p. 106). Roll Yeasted Dough into a large square 1/4 inch thick. Brush with oil and sprinkle Crumb Topping (p. 66) over dough. Roll up like a jelly roll. Cut roll into six even slices.

Place slices, cut side down, in oiled 7 × 5 × 3-inch loaf pan. (Squeeze them in if necessary.) Cover, set in a warm place until dough doubles in size. Bake in preheated 350°F oven about 45 minutes, or until lightly browned. Glaze before or after baking.

# Two Fingers

> 1 recipe Yeasted Pastry Dough (p. 106)
> Icing I (p. 60)
> Walnut Filling (p. 65)

Prepare dough. Shape and roll out into a 6 × 16 × 1/4-inch strip.

Spread dough with purée or icing. Sprinkle Walnut Filling over it. Fold lengthwise toward the center so that the two folded parts meet in the center. Then fold again to make a long four-layer roll. Cut into 1/2-inch slices. Place on a cookie sheet.

Spread the two halves of each slice slightly so they have room to expand. Cover, and set in a warm place to rise until almost doubled in size.

Bake at 350°F in a preheated oven for about 30 minutes (you may wish to turn the slices over after 20 minutes).

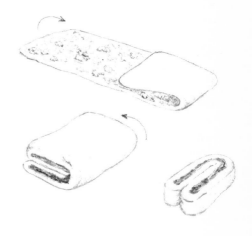

# Dumplings

> Yeasted Pastry Dough (p. 106)
> 2–3 cups fruit juice or stewed fruit
> 1 cup crushed roasted nuts

Prepare pastry dough. Shape into little balls.

Place fruit juice or stewed fruits in the bottom of a deep baking dish. Add the dumplings. (Cover, and set in a warm place to rise before baking.) Bake 1-1/2 to 2 hours covered. Do not lift the cover off during the first hour of baking time.

When all of the liquid has been absorbed, and they begin to smell sweet, remove from oven.

Garnish with nuts. Serve immediately.

## Fireside Kuchen

> 3 cups diced apples or other fruit
> 1/2 recipe Yeasted Pastry Dough (p. 106)
> 1 egg
> 1 tsp. lemon rind
> 1/2 cup Crumb Topping (p. 66)

Dice the apples. (Peel if not organic.) (If using dried fruit, first soak fruit in water to cover.) Boil and cook until soft. Squeeze out liquid, and dice. Be sure that the fruit has enough moisture to prevent it from drying up.

Preheat oven to 325°F. Oil an 11×16-inch sheet. Roll out dough, and place on sheet. Cover and let dough rise in a warm place until it becomes puffy, but not doubled in size.

Brush with a beaten egg. Arrange diced fruit on top. Combine rind and Crumb Topping, and sprinkle over fruit.

Bake in preheated oven 45 minutes, or until browned.

## Sweet Croissants

Croissants (crescent rolls) were created in Hungary about 1686, to commemorate the withdrawal of the invading Turks. Bakers working at night heard the Turks tunneling into the city and sounded the alarm which helped to defeat the Turkish troops. As a reward, the bakers were commissioned to produce a special pastry, shaped like a crescent, which is the emblem of Turkey.

> 1 recipe Yeasted Pastry Dough (p. 106)
> 3–4 cups Raisin Purée (p. 64)
> 1 cup concentrated sweetener
> 2 cups chopped almonds, walnuts or
>   pecans

Prepare dough. Flour pastry cloth. Shape and roll out dough into circle 1/8 inch thick. Cut into triangles.

Place a tsp. or less of purée on the widest side of the triangle, or spread over the whole triangle. Roll toward the opposite end and shape into crescents.

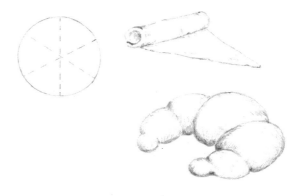

Oil a large cookie sheet. Place crescents on sheet. Cover and let rise in a warm spot until almost double in size.

Preheat the oven to 350°F. Glaze with sweetener before or after baking (p. 82). Bake 25–35 minutes, or until browned. Sprinkle nuts on top after baking.

## Fruit Stollen

I baked four of these for a Christmas dinner, and never even tasted a crumb.

> 1 cup mixed dried fruit
> 1/4 cup raisins

1-1/2 Tbsp. dry yeast
1 cup warm cider
1/4 cup concentrated sweetener
3-1/2 cups whole wheat pastry flour
1/2 cup oil
1/2 cup pecans or other chopped nuts
1 tsp. cinnamon
1/2 tsp. sea salt

Soak dried fruit and raisins in cider to cover. Squeeze out liquid and dice (set aside liquid for batter).

Dissolve yeast in warm fruit juice. Combine with sweetener. Add enough flour to form a thin batter. Cover and let rise in a warm spot until doubled in size.

Mix in other ingredients, and knead about 5–10 minutes. Punch down, and roll into an oval. Fold over lengthwise, and place on an oiled sheet or in a bread tin. Slit top. Cover and let rise.

Preheat oven to 400°F. Glaze before or after baking. Bake 10 minutes, turn down to 350°F, and bake 25–30 minutes longer. Remove from oven and place on a rack to cool.

## Doughnuts

Doughnuts were traditionally tossed in the air for children to catch on "Fat Tuesday" (mardi gras), the day before Lent.

> 1 recipe Yeasted Pastry Dough, substituting 2 Tbsp. oil for 1/2 cup (p. 106)
> 1/2 cup orange juice and rind
> Oil for deep-frying (p. 16)
> TOPPING:
> Carob Frosting (p. 61)

Add orange juice and rind to spices in dough. Prepare a soft moist dough, just firm enough to handle. Knead. Cover and chill 15 minutes.

Prepare Carob Frosting.

Roll out or pat dough to 1/2-inch thickness on a floured cloth. With a well-floured doughnut cutter, cut into rings or logs 1/2 × 4 inches.* Twist the logs gently and bring the ends together.

Place on well-oiled greaseproof paper, cover with a damp cloth and let rest 20 minutes.

Heat oil. Deep-fry about 3 minutes (1-1/2 minutes on each side) or until lightly browned. Drain and cool.

Glaze, dip into cinnamon, roasted chestnut flour, grated unsweetened coconut or crushed roasted seeds or nuts.

*Suggestions*

For more tender doughnuts, have all ingredients at room temperature.

Add dried fruits, nuts, seeds, spices to dough before resting it.

Add a few whole cloves to hot oil before deep-frying for additional flavor.

## Jelly Doughnuts

> 1 recipe Yeasted Pastry (p. 106)
> Apple butter, or any purée (p. 64)

Prepare dough. Roll out to 1/2-inch thickness. Cut into 3-inch rounds instead of rings.

Place 1 tsp. apple butter or any purée into the center of one round. Brush the edge of the round with egg white. Place another round on top. Press the edges together. Repeat with the rest of the dough. Cover and set aside 30 minutes on a lightly floured

---

* For doughnuts cut with a doughnut cutter, or a large cutter with a smaller one for the center hole.

board.

Deep-fry 3–5 minutes. Drain.

Follow directions under Doughnuts for glaze and topping.

**Apple** (*Rose family: rosaceae*)

The legend of Johnny Appleseed is well-known in America, and is still being told in many schools today. There actually was a Johnny Appleseed, whose real name was John Chapman. He collected apple seeds from cider mills, dried them and put them into tiny bags, which he gave to every person he met who was headed west.

For more than thirty five years, he travelled through Indiana, Ohio, Iowa and Illinois, planting seeds in every likely location. He was known as a bearded wanderer with an obsession for planting orchards.

## John in the Sack

2 cups chopped apples or pears
1 cup raisins
1/2 cup chopped walnuts or almonds
2 tsp. orange rind
1 tsp. cinnamon
1/2 tsp. salt
1 recipe Yeasted Pastry dough (p. 106)
Apple juice for boiling pastries

Choose fruit that has little liquid content.* Combine fruits, nuts, spices and salt. Set aside.

Prepare yeasted dough. Roll out dough. Cut out circles about 3 inches in diameter or

3 × 4-inch squares.

Place a Tbsp. of fruit filling in the center, wrap and tie securely. Place on oiled baking sheet. Cover and let rise in a warm place until almost doubled in size.

Boil juice. Drop into boiling juice and cook 20–30 minutes or until dough has been cooked.

**Alternate Methods**
1. Bake at 350°F 35–45 minutes.
2. Deep-fry (p. 16) until brown. Drain immediately.
3. Steam 30 minutes.

## Olykoecks (Hudson Valley Doughnuts)

FILLING:
4 finely chopped apples
3 Tbsp. lemon rind
1-1/2 cups raisins
2 Tbsp. cinnamon

DOUGH:
1-1/2 Tbsp. dry yeast
1/4 cup warm cider of juice
4 cups whole wheat pastry flour
1 egg
1/2 tsp. sea salt
1/2 tsp. cinnamon
1/2 tsp. ginger
1/4 cup concentrated sweetener
2 Tbsp. oil
1/4 cup cold mu tea
Apple juice to form dough
Oil for deep-frying

Chop and core apples. (Peel if not organic.) Add rind, raisins and cinnamon to apples. Mix well. Set aside.

Dilute yeast in warm liquid. Add enough flour to form a thin batter. Cover and set

---

* To remove excess liquid from fruit, cut into small pieces and sprinkle with salt. Toss lightly, allow to sit at least 30 minutes. Pour off excess liquid.

in a warm place to rise until doubled in size.

Beat egg. Add salt, cinnamon and ginger. Set aside.

Beat down batter. Add egg mixture, sweetener, oil and the rest of the flour to batter. Adjust liquid-flour content accordingly. Knead until dough is smooth and elastic. Cover and let rise in a warm place until almost doubled in size.

Punch down. Pinch off a small piece of dough and roll into a ball. Make a depression in the center and place some of the fruit mixture in the center of each ball; cover with dough. Roll into ball. Place on a floured board. Cover, set in a warm place to rest.

Heat oil. Remove doughnuts from board and roll again to make them round. Drop into hot oil and deep-fry about 5 minutes, rotating each ball after first 2-1/2 minutes. Drain.

Dust with chestnut flour or cinnamon. Serve immediately.

## Variation

Substitute any fresh fruit in season or any dried fruit for apples.

## Miso Tahini Twist

    1/4 cup lukewarm water
    1 Tbsp. yeast
    1/2 cup concentrated sweetener
    1/3 cup oil
    2 cups whole wheat pastry flour
    1/4 tsp. sea salt
FILLING:
    1/4 cup tahini
    1/4 cup miso
    1/4 cup concentrated sweetener
    1 Tbsp. orange rind

Place water in bowl and sprinkle yeast over it. Add concentrated sweetener and oil, and mix until creamy. Cover and place in a warm spot to bubble.

Add flour and salt, stirring briskly until mixture begins to thicken and forms a dough. Knead mixture 10 minutes. (Adjust liquid.) Cover and set in a warm place to rise (30–40 minutes).

*Filling*

Combine all filling ingredients together and mix until smooth paste forms. (Add small amount of warm liquid to help cream.)

*Rolling out*

Divide dough into quarters. Keep unused sections covered with a damp cloth.

Roll dough into large square 1/4 inch thick. Brush with oil and spread filling over dough. Roll up very tightly into a thin log.

Continue until four logs are formed.

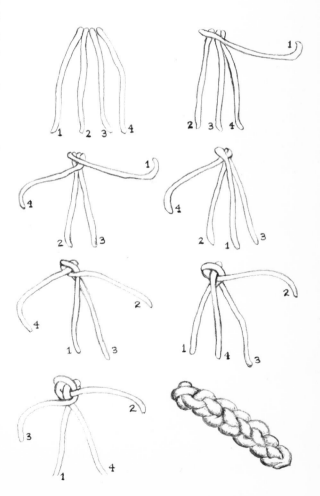

Braid strips together to make loaf. Place in oiled and floured loaf tin or on baking sheet. Cover and set in a warm spot until dough doubles in size.

Preheat oven to 350°F. Brush dough with egg wash before baking (p. 82), or concentrated sweetener just after baking.

## Puff Pies

> 1 recipe Yeasted Pastry Dough (p. 106)
> FILLING:
> 2 cups date purée (p. 64)
> 1/2 cup crushed walnuts
> 1 Tbsp. orange rind
> Oil for deep-frying
> Roasted chestnut flour or cinnamon
>     for dusting

Sprinkle arrowroot flour on rolling surface. Combine purée, nuts and rind.

Roll out dough to 1/4-inch thickness and cut out 3-inch circles. Place a spoonful of filling in the center of one of the circles. Moisten the edge of the dough all around the filling with water or egg. Place another circle on top, and press edges firmly together. Repeat until all dough is used. Cover and set in a warm place for about 20 minutes. Heat oil. Deep-fry until browned on both sides. Drain, and sprinkle with roasted chestnut flour or cinnamon while still warm.

## Saucers

> 1 recipe Yeasted Pastry Dough (p. 106)
> 3–4 cups Chestnut Cream (p. 144)
> 1 cup concentrated sweetener
> 2–3 tsp. cinnamon

Prepare dough. Flour surface and roll out dough 1/4 inch thick. Cut out circles 4–6 inches in diameter.

Oil baking tray. Place half of the circles on sheet. Spread with filling, leaving 1/2

inch all around edges of circle. Using a small knife or razor blade, score remaining circles with arcs radiating from the center of the circle. Place over filling. Press edges to seal in filling.

Cover and set in a warm place to rise until almost double in size. Brush top with concentrated sweetener, and sprinkle on cinnamon.

Preheat oven to 350°F. Bake 45–60 minutes or until pastry is browned.

**Variations**
Add 2 tsp. orange rind to dough.

Substitute any vegetable or cream filling.

Unyeasted pastry dough may be substituted for yeasted dough (p. 79).

**Orange** (*Citrus sinensis*)
Oranges are given their color by cold weather. They have an outer skin that is green from chlorophyll. The thin membrane breaks down in cold weather, destroying the chlorophyll and turning the orange its characteristic color. The fruit is not necessarily ripe, even if it is orange.

When oranges are put into the store to be sold, they have to be orange, otherwise they will not sell. Ethylene gas is used to turn a green fruit orange, or an orange fruit brighter.

Sometimes a wax coating is applied to the skin, to prevent the orange from shrivelling up. If too much wax is applied, the orange will not be able to breathe and will "suffocate" and lose some of its taste.

## Hamentaschen

Purim celebrates the victory of the beautiful Queen Esther over the evil Haman. Purim was the most exciting holiday on the Jewish calendar. It meant helping my mother bake the traditional Hamentaschen, poppy seed or prune-filled triangles of pastry, that are said to represent Haman's hat.

1 recipe Yeasted Pastry Dough (p. 106)
PRUNE RAISIN FILLING:
1 lb. prunes
1 cup sultanas
1/4 tsp. sea salt
Juice and rind of 1/2 orange
2 Tbsp. lemon rind
1/2 cup chopped roasted almonds

Soak prunes and sultanas in water to cover for 10 minutes. Bring to a boil, add sea salt, and boil down until there is no more liquid left. Remove pits from prunes.

Blend cooked fruit together with the rest of the ingredients except almonds. Fold in nuts.

Roll out dough to 1/4-inch thickness. Cut into squares about 4×4 inches.

Make a depression in the center of each square. Spoon in 1 Tbsp. filling. Pinch each corner together, leaving about 1-1/2 inches of the filling exposed.

Sprinkle with cinnamon. Place on oiled sheet, cover and set in a warm spot to rise until pastry has almost doubled in size.

Glaze before or after baking (p. 82). Bake in a preheated 350°F oven 30–45 minutes, or until browned.

## Schnecken

Prepare Yeasted Pastry Dough (p. 106). Set aside.

Combine 1/4 cup oil with 2 Tbsp. maple syrup. Oil muffin tins or cupcake tins with this mixture. Place a few pecans in each cup.

Roll dough into a long rectangle 1/4 inch thick. Sprinkle Crumb Topping (p. 66), raisins, and nuts over dough. Roll up dough tightly like jelly roll, sealing the seam with water or egg.

Stretch out the roll if it is too thick for the tins, or compress it if it is too thin. Slice into small pieces and fill the cups halfway.

Cover, set in a warm place until dough doubles in size.

Bake in preheated 350°F oven about 25–30 minutes, or until lightly browned.

Turn pans upside-down on cake rack immediately (place cookie sheet underneath pan to catch the drippings) to remove schnecken and allow glaze to drip over the sides.

## Sweet Buns

1 recipe Yeasted Pastry Dough (p. 106)
1 cup soaked raisins
1/2 cup concentrated sweetener

Follow directions for Yeasted Pastry Dough, adding raisins after first rise. Cut off small pieces of dough and shape.

Place in oiled cupcake tins after shaping, cover, and let rise until almost doubled in size.

Preheat oven to 350°F. Bake 20–30 minutes or until browned. (Tap on bottom and top of bun. When it sounds hollow, it is done.)

Remove from oven, brush with concentrated sweetener and chill immediately.

### Variations

Bring apple juice to a boil, add 4 Tbsp. grain coffee (p. 20). Cool juice to warm before adding yeast. Add 1 tsp. ginger to dry mixture before adding oil.

Add 1 cup roasted chopped walnuts, almonds or pecans to flour mixture.

Add juice and rind of 1 grated orange to flour mixture after the first rise.

## Tofu Crumb Roll

YEASTED PASTRY DOUGH:
   1 Tbsp. dry yeast
   3/4–1-1/2 cups apple juice or cider
   2–4 Tbsp. concentrated sweetener
   1 tsp. vanilla
   3-1/2 whole wheat pastry flour
   1/2 tsp. sea salt
   2 tsp. cinnamon
   1 Tbsp. orange or lemon rind
   1/2 cup oil
FILLING:
   3 cups Tofu Crumb Filling (p. 65)
   3–4 Tbsp. tahini

Prepare Tofu Crumb Filling. Set aside.

Dissolve yeast in 1/2 cup lukewarm apple juice or cider; add sweetener here if desired. Stir and set aside 5 minutes or until mixture bubbles.

Add enough flour to form a thin batter. Beat until smooth and not lumpy. Clean down the sides of the bowl with a rubber spatula. Cover and let rise in a warm spot until it is almost doubled in size. Beat in oil and vanilla. Combine the rest of the dry ingredients, reserving 1/2 cup of flour, and beat into yeasted mixture until it is too hard to beat. Add only enough apple juice or cider to form a soft sticky dough.

Knead dough on a lightly floured surface, kneading in the reserved flour if necessary to make the dough perfectly smooth. Place in an oiled bowl, cover and let rise in a warm spot until doubled in size. (After rising, it should feel soft and puffy.)

Roll out dough to 1/4-inch thickness.

Spread tahini and sprinkle Tofu Crumb Filling evenly over dough. Roll up into jelly roll.

Cut roll in half. Place each loaf in an oiled 9 × 5 × 3-inch loaf pan. Cover, set in a warm place until dough doubles in size. Bake in preheated 350°F oven 45 minutes or until browned.

Glaze before or after baking (p. 82).

## Danish Ring

Prepare Yeasted Pastry Dough (p. 106). Roll out dough into a rectangle approximately 6 × 20 × 1/4 inches.

Spread dough with date purée (p. 64). Fold to make strip one third of its previous width. Roll with a rolling pin to lengthen and flatten.

Cut into dough with a knife, making three incisions lengthwise, equally spaced apart, almost the entire length of the strip, leaving 1 inch uncut at both ends. Take one end in each hand. Turn and twist the ends in opposite directions to form a long twist, stretching dough slightly as you twist.

Hold ends, shaping into a ring. Cross the ends, and press them firmly together. Press down with thumbs or hand on crossed ends, and flip over the ring to conceal the ends.

Place on oiled baking tray. Cover. Set in a warm place until dough doubles in size.

Bake in a preheated 350°F oven 30–40 minutes.

## Upside-down Pecan Swirls

1 recipe Yeasted Pastry Dough (p. 106)
3–4 cups Apricot Purée (p. 64)
2–3 cups Crumb Topping (p. 66)
1 tsp. vanilla
1/2–1 cup sweetener
Roasted pecan halves

Follow rolling and shaping directions for Cinnamon Rolls (p. 109).

Pour sweetener into oiled cupcake tins. Place pecans in tins. Cut dough into 1-inch slices. Sprinkle over pecans.

Cover, and let rise till almost doubled in size.

Preheat oven to 350°F. Bake 25–30 minutes, or until brown.

# 7. MUNCHIES: Cookies and Slices

Fill the cookie jar with a variety of shapes that complement each other in texture and flavor. You may want to experiment using various-shaped cookie cutters, natural colorings, flavorings and techniques, as well as combining different flours to make rolled, chewy, nut, drop, icebox cookies or bars.

If so, see the information on flour (p. 19). It is always a good idea to sample the cookie batter or dough before baking, and adjust the seasoning to taste. Bake extra-special cookies for the holidays, and keep the jar filled with tasty treats all year round, satisfying everyone's sweet tooth.

## Forget Me Knots

1. The amount of liquid necessary for each recipe will differ each time, according to the moisture in the flour and the room, the size of eggs and the general weather of the day.
2. Always preheat the oven.

3. Use unrefined corn-germ or corn oil for light, flaky cookies.

4. In making any kind of cookie, never beat or knead the dough after the flour has been added or the cookies may be tough. Eggs used in dough should be at room temperature.

5. Do not roll dough in excessive amounts of flour. Roll out cookie dough on a lightly floured board, or between two sheets of wax paper, which are placed on a lightly floured board. This technique usually produces more tender cookies.

6. Keep the dough covered and chilled until you roll it.

7. Dust cookie cutters with flour or cinnamon before using them. Use glasses, bowls, cups etc., for unusual designs.

8. Usually, cookie sheets do not have to be oiled.

9. Cookie sheets may be oiled with beeswax or use deep-frying oil in place of corn or sesame oil.

10. Use a flat baking sheet or the bottom of a reversed baking pan, so that the heat can circulate directly and evenly over the cookie tops.

11. Dark cookie sheets absorb heat, and cookies may brown more on the bottom. Good cookie sheets have shiny baking surfaces, and specially dulled bottoms to produce more even browning.

12. A pan with high sides will deflect the heat and make the cookies difficult to remove after baking.

13. A baking or cookie sheet should be at least 2 inches shorter and narrower than the oven rack, so that the air can circulate around it.

14. Cookie sheets should always be cold when you put the cookies on them so the cookies will not lose their shape.

15. Transfer rolled or molded cookies from rolling surface to cookie sheet with a spatula.

16. Drop cookies tend to spread more than other cookies, so leave 2 inches between them. Try to make them the same size, so they will be done at the same time.

17. Watch cookies carefully because ovens tend to overheat. The later batches tend to cook more quickly.

18. When a cookie sheet is partially filled, the heat is drawn to the area where the cookies lie, and the cookies may burn on the bottom before they are baked. If there is not enough batter or dough to fill a cookie sheet, use a reversed pie pan or small baking tin instead.

19. When baking cookies, place sheet on only one rack. If two racks are used, the heat circulates unevenly so that the bottoms of the cookies on the lower rack and the tops of the cookies on the upper rack brown too quickly.

20. During baking, turn the cookie sheets around for a more even baking.

21. After baking, remove the cookies from the sheet immediately, or they will continue to cook.

22. Always cool cookies spread out on a rack, and not overlapping.

23. When deep-frying cookies, seeds and nuts have a tendency to separate from the batter or dough unless finely ground.

24. *Do not store crisp and soft cookies together*.

25. Store crisp cookies in a jar with a loose-fitting cover in a cool place. If they soften, put them in a slow oven for five minutes before serving.

26. Keep soft cookies moist by storing them in a cool place in a covered jar. If cookies dry out, put a piece of bread, an apple, an orange or a clove-studded lemon in the jar with them to help maintain the moisture.

# Recipes

## Shades of Things to Come

### Bull's Eye

Prepare two doughs, one plain, one dark. (Add grain coffee or raisin purée for dark color.) Form a quarter of the dark dough into a log 1 inch thick and 6 inches long. Wrap in wax paper and chill 2 hours.

Roll three quarters of the plain dough into a 4×6 inch rectangle, 1/4 inch thick, and roll around dark dough. Reverse with the remaining dough. Wrap in paper and chill at least 2 hours.

Slice into 1/2-inch pieces and bake at 350°F 12–15 minutes.

### Half and Half

Prepare two logs, one plain, one dark (see Bull's Eye, above). Wrap in wax paper and chill.

Cut lengthwise through the center of each log. Brush surfaces with sweetener and press together, the plain against the dark. Wrap in wax paper and chill at least 2 hours.

Slice 1/4–1/2 inch thick and bake at 350°F 12–15 minutes (see Rolled Cookies, p. 123).

### Crisscross

Prepare Half and Half cookie logs. Cut lengthwise through the center. Brush cut surface with sweetener. Turn one of the halves around and place it end to end with the other half. Press together. Wrap and chill at least 2 hours.

Slice 1/4 to 1/2 inch thick and bake at 350°F 12–15 minutes (see Rolled Cookies, p. 123).

## Marble Effect

*A.* Prepare a few logs of different colors. Wrap and chill. Take off small pieces from each log, and roll them out together in one large circle. Cut with cookie cutter.

*B.* Combine a few pieces from each color dough, shape into one log, wrap and chill at least 4 hours. Slice into 1/4-inch cookies. Place on an unoiled sheet, and bake at 375°F 10–12 minutes.

## Pinwheels

> 1-1/2 cups whole wheat pastry flour
> 2 cups chestnut, brown rice or sweet brown rice flour
> 1 Tbsp. orange rind or mint
> 1/2 tsp. sea salt
> 1/2 cup oil
> 1/2 cup concentrated sweetener
> Vanilla
> 1 egg (optional)
> Apple juice or cider if necessary
> 1/3 cup grain coffee (1 tsp. cloves plus 1/3 cup flour may be subtituted for grain coffee)

Combine dry ingredients, except grain coffee. Cut oil in until mixture resembles tiny bread crumbs. Add sweetener, vanilla and beaten egg. Mix with wooden spoon.

Divide mixture in half. Add grain coffee to one half. Add juice or cider to each mixture until two doughs are formed.

Roll out light dough into a large rectangle between two sheets of greaseproof paper. Roll dark rectangle the same way. Remove paper, and invert dark dough on light dough. Roll up like a jelly roll. Wrap in wax paper, sealing the ends well. Chill at least 1 hour.

Preheat oven to 350°F. Slice 1/2 inch thick. Bake 10–12 minutes, or until lightly browned.

## Variation

Substitute ingredients for Rolled Cookies.

Follow directions for Pinwheels.

## Rolled Cookies

Holiday cookies usually take a shape associated with the occasion being celebrated: Christmas trees for Christmas, rabbits for Easter, hearts for Valentine's Day. By using special cookie cutters to form such shapes as these, any holiday cookies can be made.

The trick to making successful cookies is simple. The dough must not be too soft. Excess flour must not be added when rolling out. Too much flour can make the cookie too tough to eat.

*Helpful hints*
1. Divide large amounts of dough into a few pieces.
2. Cookie doughs that contain neither sweeteners nor eggs may be less firm than sweetened dough. Wrap and chill overnight, and roll out dough on greaseproof paper floured with arrowroot.
3. Substituting chestnut flour or brown rice flour for half of the whole wheat pastry flour will also produce a firmer dough.
4. Cookie dough that contain sweeteners can be chilled a shorter length of time than non-sweetened doughs. Extra-long chilling can make this dough too firm and difficult to roll out. (Cookie dough that contains both sweeteners and eggs can be chilled longer.) If dough becomes too firm, unwrap and let sit at room temperature until easier to work with (about 1 hour).
5. Roll out on a floured surface or between two sheets of greaseproof paper (see p. 80).
6. Flour cookie cutters only if the dough is soft and sticky.

7. If the dough is not too floury; reroll and use the scraps.

**Carrot** (*Daucus carota*)

Carrots known to the Romans and the Greeks are now cultivated in every part of the world. They are a rich source of vitamin A and contain a great deal of natural sugar. There is another kind of carrot, known to many as "wild carrot," that grows wild all over the countryside. This is also an edible species, with a small, pale-colored root, but there are plants resembling the carrot which are poisonous, so be careful. Because of the high amount of sugar that they contain, carrots are a wonderful source of natural sweetness that can be used in any dessert.

## Rolled Cookies

1/2 cup cold oil
1 tsp. vanilla
1/4 cup concentrated sweetener
3/4–1 cup cold liquid
3/4 tsp. salt
1 tsp. cinnamon
3/4 tsp. dry ginger
1 cup brown rice flour
2 cups whole wheat pastry flour
1 egg (for glazing)

Mix together oil, vanilla, sweetener and liquid, and stir until smooth. Sift dry ingredients together and add the liquid mixture, mixing with a wooden spoon until a ball of dough begins to form. Divide into three pieces. Cover and chill at least 60 minutes before rolling. While shaping, keep unused dough covered with a damp cloth until ready to use.

Preheat oven to 375°F.

Roll out dough to 1/4-inch thickness. Cut the cookies with any shape cutters; brush with beaten egg and sprinkle with one of the following: chopped nuts, cinnamon, or sesame seeds.

Place cookies on a sheet and bake 10–15 minutes, or until crisp. Place on a rack to cool.

If dough becomes too soft and warm after cutting, cover sheet and chill about 30 minutes before baking; this will make the cookies more crisp.

### Alternate Method

Follow directions for Rolled Cookies. Experiment by shaping the dough into different form—logs, squares, balls, etc.

Heat oil in a deep pot (p. 16). Deep-fry cookies until lightly browned. Drain on paper towels or paper bags before serving.

### Variations for Rolled Cookies

*Lemon-walnut Cookies:* Add grated rind, juice of 1/2 lemon and 1/2 cup crushed walnuts to dry ingredients.

*Orange-almond Cookies:* Add grated rind and juice of 1/2 orange and 1/2 cup crushed almonds. (Decrease oil by 1/4 cup.)

*Poppy-seed-lemon Cookies:* Add 1 cup poppy seeds to mixing bowl before adding flour. Add grated rind and juice of 1/2 lemon to liquid mixture.

*Lemon-walnut-mint Cookies:* Follow directions for Lemon-walnut Cookies, adding 2–3 tsp. mint to dry mixture before combining with liquid.

*Mint-walnut Cookies:* Follow directions

for Rolled Cookies. Add 1 tsp. mint to dry ingredients, and press in crushed walnuts.

*Sweet Orange-mint Cookies:* Follow directions for Rolled Cookies, substituting 1 Tbsp. mint for ginger, and adding orange rind to taste to dry ingredients.

*Sesame-mint Cookies:* Add 1 Tbsp. mint and 1/2 cup roasted sesame seeds to oil mixture before adding dry ingredients.

*Sweet Mint Drops:* Substitute 1 Tbsp. mint for ginger, and add enough apple juice or cider to form a stiff batter. Drop onto cookie sheet, and bake 10–15 minutes, or until brown.

*Wafers:* Dip a piece of cheesecloth in water, wring it out and tie it securely around the bottom of a glass. Press into cookie dough.

## Plainly Simple Rainbows

One Thanksgiving I was invited to Michio and Aveline Kushi's house for dinner. I baked an assortment of cookies (Half and Half, Crisscross and Rainbows), placed them individually in a cookie box for the lady of the house.

> 2 cups whole wheat pastry flour
> 1 cup chestnut flour
> 1 tsp. sea salt
> 1/2 cup oil
> 2 tsp. vanilla
> COLORS
> 1/4 cup beet juice
> 1/4 cup carrot purée
> 1/4 cup instant grain coffee
> 1/4 cup carob powder

Sift flour. Place flour and salt in a mixing bowl. Cut oil into flour mixture until it looks like tiny bread crumbs. Add vanilla. Divide mixture into four equal portions and place in separate mixing bowls.

Add one color to each bowl, mixing with a wooden spoon until a ball of dough begins to form (add apple juice or cider if the mixture is too dry).

Roll out each piece of dough between two sheets of greaseproof paper into a rectangle. Chill 2 hours.

Cut each piece of dough in half lengthwise, cutting through the paper. Peel off top sheets.

Brush the top of one strip with sweetener. Place another strip, paper side up, on top.

Peel off paper.

Repeat procedure with the remaining dough strips, alternating colors, to make eight layers.

Press lightly together. Cut stack lengthwise to make two narrow stacks. Wrap in paper and chill 30 minutes.

Preheat oven to 375°F. Cut dough into 1-inch slices. Bake 10–15 minutes or until lightly browned on bottom.

**Carob** (*Ceratonia siliqua*)
In it's appearance, the tree which bears the carob pod, looks very much like an apple tree with small flowers. It is a dark evergreen tree, which grows wild in the countries that border the Mediterranean sea and on the islands off the east coast of Spain. The carob grows a brown, leathery pod, 4 to 10 inches long. It is the pod that contains a sticky pulp that is fed to horses and cattle and sometimes eaten by people. Supposedly carob is said to have been eaten by John the Baptist when he lived in the wilderness, and is sometimes referred to as "Saint John's Bread."

## Cookie Canes

    3 cups whole wheat pastry flour
    1/2 tsp. sea salt
    3 tsp. dried mint
    2 Tbsp. carob powder
    1/2 cup concentrated sweetener
    2 tsp. vanilla
    1/2 cup oil
    2 eggs
    1/4 cup beet juice
    Apple juice to form dough

Prepare two mixing bowls, divide the first three ingredients in half and sift into separate bowls. Add carob to one.

Divide the next three ingredients in half, beat and add to each bowl of sifted flour.

Whisk each egg separately. Add beet juice to one egg, mixing well. Add beaten egg to carob mixture, and beetroot egg to other mixture. Form two soft doughs, using apple juice if necessary.

Roll each dough into a log and divide into six pieces. Cover. Roll out two pieces, one of each color into a log 18 inches long. Place strips side by side, pressing the ends together, and twist. Place on unoiled sheet about 1 inch apart, and bend the tops of the twists into a cane shape.

Bake in preheated 350°F oven 15–20 minutes or until almost firm and browned on the bottom. Glaze with concentrated sweetener immediately after removing from oven.

If you want to hang them on the tree, insert wooden or metal skewer into the end of the curved part of the cane before baking to form a hole for the string.

## Diamonds

    1/4 cup concentrated sweetener
    1/4 cup plus 2 Tbsp. oil
    Juice and rind of 1/2 lemon
    Juice and rind of 1/2 orange
    1 cup slivered almonds
    1 Tbsp. cinnamon
    1 tsp. cardamon
    1/2 tsp. sea salt
    1-1/2 cups sifted whole wheat pastry flour
    1/4 cup sifted corn flour
    Apple juice to form dough

Beat together sweetener and oil until creamy. Add next three ingredients.

Sift dry ingredients. Combine with first mixture and add enough apple juice to form a dough.

Shape into rectangle and roll out to 1/2-inch thickness on oiled greaseproof paper. Place paper and dough onto baking sheet. Cut halfway into dough, forming diamonds.

Bake in preheated 325°F oven 20–25 minutes or until lightly browned and almost firm. Remove from pan and cool on rack. (Peel off paper before cooling.) Glaze with concentrated sweetener immediately.

## Joe Froggers

Joe Froggers is the name of a cookie that the fisherman of Marblehead took with them on their long trips. These big, fat cookies are named after the big, fat frogs that sit on top of lily pads in New England ponds.

    4 cups whole wheat pastry flour
    1 Tbsp. cinnamon
    1 tsp. ginger
    1 tsp. cloves
    1/4 tsp. coriander
    1/2 tsp. sea salt
    1/4 cup instant grain coffee
    3/4 cup oil
    1/2 cup concentrated sweetener

2 tsp. vanilla
1/2–1 cup apple juice

Combine first seven ingredients together. Set aside.

Whisk together all liquid ingredients. Sift dry ingredients, add beaten liquid mixture and stir until a soft dough is formed. (Adjust liquid content accordingly.) Wrap in paper and chill at least 1 hour.

Roll out on greaseproof paper to 1/2-inch thickness. Cut with 4-inch cookie cutter or glass.

Place on sheet, and bake in 375°F preheated oven 12–15 minutes or until lightly browned and almost firm. Glaze with concentrated sweetener immediately after removing from oven.

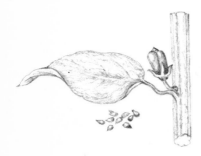

**Sesame** (*Sesamum indicum*)
The sesame was originally from Africa; although today it is grown in Mexico, California, and other tropical or subtropical climates.

The plant grows up to 6 feet high, taking 3 to 5 months to mature. The different varieties have many flowers, such as white, pink or mauve. When harvested, the whole plants are cut and stacked upright to dry. As they dry, the seed capsules split open and the plants are usually turned upside-down and shaken out onto a cloth. These seeds contain 45 to 50 percent oil, which is used in various ways in desserts. The seeds can be used for nut butters and for decoration in cooking and baking.

# Sesame Seed Biscuits

1 cup sesame seeds

1-1/2 cups whole wheat pastry flour
1 tsp cinnamon
1/2 tsp sea salt
1 cup rolled oats
1/2 cup cold oil
1/2–1 cup apple juice
2 Tbsp. tahini
1 tsp. vanilla

Lightly roast sesame seeds in a dry skillet until they just begin to pop. Crush immediately. (Use blender or *suribachi*\*.)

Combine next three ingredients and sift. Add rolled oats and sesame seeds. Set aside.

Beat next four ingredients together until creamy. Add wet mixture to dry mixture and stir until ball of dough forms. (Adjust liquid-flour content.)

Roll dough into log, wrap in paper, and chill 30 minutes or until firm.

Preheat oven to 400°F and oil cookie sheets. Slice off into 1/2-inch pieces, or roll out to 1/4-inch thickness and cut out different shapes with cutter. (Keep dough refrigerated until using.)

Bake 10–15 minutes or until slightly browned on bottom and almost firm. Remove from pan, brush with glaze if desired.

**Variation**
Substitute any crushed nut or seed for sesame seeds. Add 1 tsp. ginger to dry ingredients.

## Sweet Mint Cookies

1/4–1/2 cup apple juice or cider
2 Tbsp. peanut butter
1/2 cup concentrated sweetener
1 tsp. lemon rind

---

\* *Suribachi*—A *suribachi* is a bowl with ridges on the inside. It is used to crush seeds, nuts and cream salad dressings. A pestle cracks or crushes the ingredients. Much like a mortor and pestle, but more versatile.

1 tsp. orange rind
1 Tbsp. mint
3/4 tsp. ginger
1 tsp. cinnamon
1 cup crushed roasted peanuts
2-1/4 cups whole wheat pastry flour
1/2 cup millet flour
1/2 tsp. sea salt

Blend juice or cider, peanut butter, and concentrated sweetener together. Heat in saucepan, add rinds, mint and spices. Cool.

Roast and crush nuts. Combine with flour and salt, and gradually stir in wet mixture until a ball of dough forms. (Adjust liquid content.) Wrap and chill.

Preheat oven to 350°F and oil cookie sheets. Roll out dough to 1/2-inch thickness, cut into shapes and bake 20–25 minutes or until lightly browned. Remove and brush with concentrated sweetener.

## Christmas Sandwiches

1 cup brown rice flour
2 cups whole wheat pastry flour
1 tsp. cinnamon
1/2 tsp. coriander
1/2 tsp. sea salt
1/2 cup concentrated sweetener
3 eggs
3/4 cup corn oil
1 tsp. vanilla
TAHINI-POPPY FILLING:
1/3 cup poppy seeds
2/3 cup raisins
1/4 tsp sea salt
2 Tbsp. grain coffee
1 cup apple juice or cider
1/2 cup tahini
1 tsp. lemon rind
1 tsp. cinnamon

Sift first five ingredients together. Set aside. Beat sweetener and eggs together until creamy. Slowly drip in oil and continue beating until fully absorbed. Add vanilla.

Place dry ingredients on board. Make a well in the center, and put egg mixture in. Begin to mix dry ingredients toward center incorporating both together until dough forms. (Adjust liquid content accordingly.) Cover and chill 30 minutes.

*Tahini-poppy filling*

Cook poppy seeds, raisins, sea salt, grain coffee and apple juice or cider together for 10–15 minutes, or until most of the liquid has evaporated.

Place mixture in a blender, add remaining ingredients and blend until creamy. (You may have to add more liquid to get a creamy consistency.) Set aside.

Preheat oven to 350°F and oil cookie sheets. Roll out dough to 1/4 inch thickness and cut out with cookie cutters. Bake 15–20 minutes or until bottom is lightly browned. Glaze and cool on rack. Spread filling in between and sandwich together.

### Variations

Add 2 Tbsp. instant grain coffee to dry ingredients. Press center of cookie with thumb and insert drop of fruit purée or halved almond before baking.

*Odds and ends*

Use any leftover dough (pies, cookies, strudel, pastries). Roll out on greaseproof paper and cut with cutters into different shapes.

Preheat oven to 350°F, place on oiled sheet and bake 10 minutes. Brush with shoyu and bake another 5–10 minutes.

*Charlotte suggestion*

Oil mold. Cool finger shaped (p. 129) biscuits and place in mold all around the sides. Fill mold with chestnut cream or any creamy filling that contains agar-agar so that it jells.

# Molded Cookies

German and Danish cookies are so appealing because they are pressed with wooden molds or rollers which have quaint designs and shapes carved into them.

No matter what kind of technique you use for molding—pastry bags, cookie presses, wooden molds, carved rollers or just your hands—you won't be able to make them as quickly as they are eaten.

## Almond Kisses

> 3 Tbsp. almond butter
> 1/4 cup concentrated sweetener
> 2 egg whites
> 1 tsp. vanilla
> 1/2 cup arrowroot flour
> 3/4–1 cup whole wheat pastry flour
> 1/4 tsp. sea salt
> 1-1/4 cup ground almonds
> Blanched almond halves (p. 16)

Beat together almond butter and sweetener until creamy and light. Beat egg whites until stiff peaks form. Fold in nut-butter combination very gently. Add vanilla.

Sift flours and sea salt together and add to first mixture. Add ground almonds. Stir gently, until a smooth, moist dough is formed.

Using a pastry bag and medium size tube (p. 57), fill the bag with cookie dough and press out into 2-inch kisses on oiled sheet (p. 58), leaving about 2 inches between each one. Press almond halves into the center of each cookie.

Bake in preheated 400°F oven 10–12 minutes or until edges begin to lightly brown. Cool on rack.

**Sweet Chestnut** (*Castanea sativa*)
Originally from southern Europe, the chestnut tree has been planted in many different parts of the world.

Chestnuts grow on moderately large trees, characterised by alternate deciduous leaves with bristle-tipped margins. Their small, inconspicuous unisexual flowers are born in catkins. The fruit, a nut, born in clusters of two or three, is enclosed in a leathery husk, clothed with multibranched spines. Both the wood and the bark of the tree contain tannin, a chemical complex which is extracted in commercial quantities and used in converting rawhides into leather.

The European or Spanish chestnut (called marron) is probably the most important species. It grows in southern Europe as well as North Africa, southern Asia, England and India. During the nineteenth century, it became widely established and is still frequently encountered in California and the Pacific Northwest.

The largest nuts are eaten raw, boiled or roasted. Smaller ones are dried and milled into flour. The smallest nuts are fed to livestock.

Chestnuts are used in soups, stuffings and desserts, as well as roasted and eaten hot from the oven.

## Chestnut Balls

> 1 cup sweet brown rice or brown rice
>    flour
> 1/2 cup chestnut flour
> 4 Tbsp. oil
> 1/4 tsp. sea salt
> 1 tsp. vanilla
> 1/4 cup concentrated sweetener
> 2 Tbsp. tahini
> 1/4–1/2 cup apple juice

Roast the flours separately in oil until they begin to smell sweet and slightly brown. Cool.

Sift flour and salt together. Combine vanilla, sweetener tahini and 1/4 cup juice together. Stir until creamy. Stir into dry mixture and add more liquid if necessary until mixture begins to stick together.

Prepare steamer (p. 15). Shape mixture into little balls. Cover and steam 10 minutes. Cool on rack before serving. Roll in crushed, roasted nuts or carob flour, for added effect.

### Alternate Method

Roll mixture into log. Cut into even pieces, press out and place on oiled sheet. Bake at 375°F 10–12 minutes or until lightly browned.

### Fingers

> 1 recipe Rolled Cookies (p. 123)
> Crushed nuts

Follow directions for Rolled Cookies. Shape dough into fingers, wrap individually in paper and chill overnight. Preheat oven to 375°F.

Roll fingers in crushed nuts and place on unoiled sheet. Bake 10–12 minutes or until lightly browned. (Brush fingers with egg white if nuts do not adhere to dough.)

### Variation

Shape dough into long, thin rolls, and twist into pretzel shape. Brush with egg yolk and bake 15–20 minutes.

### Spirals

> 1/4 cup oil
> 1/4 cup concentrated sweetener
> 2 egg whites
> 1 tsp. vanilla
> 1-1/4 cups sifted whole wheat flour
> 1/4 tsp. sea salt

Combine oil and sweetener, beating well until creamy. Separate eggs and beat white until stiff peaks form. Add vanilla and combine with oil and sweetener mixture.

Sift flour and salt together, and fold into egg mixture. Stir until a very thick, moist dough is formed.

Fill pastry bag and press out into spiral shapes on oiled sheet. Leave 2 inches between cookies for expansion.

Bake 8–12 minutes in preheated 400°F oven.

### Variations

1. Add 2 Tbsp. instant grain coffee to oil-sweetener combination before folding in flour.
2. Add 1 Tbsp. cinnamon and 3/4 tsp. ginger to flour before sifting.

## Sesame Almond Flakes

> 4 Tbsp. sesame butter
> 1/4 cup concentrated sweetener
> 1/4 cup oil
> 1 egg
> 1-1/2 cups sifted whole wheat pastry flour
> 1/4 cup cornmeal
> 1 Tbsp. lemon rind
> 1/4 tsp. sea salt
> Apple juice to form dough

Combine sesame butter, sweetener and oil. Beat until thick and creamy. Keep beating and drop in egg. Continue beating until smooth. Sift flour, add cornmeal, rind and salt, and fold into first mixture. Add juice if necessary to form soft dough.

Preheat oven to 375°F. Shape dough into little balls, place on unoiled sheet and press with 1/2 almond in center. Bake 10–15 minutes or until almost firm.

## Lemon Balls

> 1/4 cup concentrated sweetener
> 1 Tbsp. corn oil
> 2 Tbsp. lemon juice
> 2 cups whole wheat pastry flour
> 1 Tbsp. lemon rind
> 1/4 cup crushed peanuts
> 1/2 tsp. salt
> 1 tsp. cardamon
> Apple juice to form dough
> Oil for deep-frying

Combine first three ingredients together. Whisk until well combined.

Place flour, rind, crushed nuts, salt and cardamon in mixing bowl, and combine with first mixture. Stir well. Add enough apple juice to form a soft dough. Roll out into a log, cut into equal sections and roll into balls.

Heat oil and deep-fry until lightly browned. Drain well and roll in cinnamon, roasted chestnut or soybean flour while still warm.

**Alternate Method**

Roll dough into a log, wrap in wax paper and chill at least 60 minutes. Remove from refrigerator, cut into 1/4-inch pieces and bake at 350°F 10–12 minutes.

# Drop Cookies

Most drop cookies are made by the teaspoon or tablespoon method. Some batters fall easily from the spoon, expanding and flattening while baking. When chilled before baking, some of these batters can actually be formed into balls or logs and baked as is, or flattened with a lightly oiled glass or biscuit cutter.

Stiffer doughs can be shaped and formed through a pastry bag, fitted with a large plain star or ribbon-type tube (p. 56). Make sure that the tube is large enough to allowed chopped fruits and nuts or seeds to pass through easily.

*Pastry bag method*

Fill pastry bag half full of batter. Seal in the batter by twisting the top of the bag (p. 57).

Line the cookie sheets with greaseproof paper. Oil paper.

Hold the bag vertically with the tip of the tube 1/2 inch away from the cookie sheet, and press out rounds, kisses or strips of batter directly onto paper. Cut off dough with wet knife or quick upward movement.

## Lemon Currant Cookies

> 1 cup rolled oats or barley
> 1/2 cup whole wheat pastry flour
> 1/2 cup brown rice flour
> 1/4 cup crushed sesame seeds
> 1 Tbsp. lemon rind
> 2 tsp. cinnamon
> 1/2 tsp. sea salt

1/2 cup chopped currants
1/4–1/2 cup apple juice
1/2 cup concentrated sweetener
1/2 cup corn oil
1 tsp. vanilla

Roast oats or barley until lightly browned in unoiled skillet. Combine with next seven ingredients.

Heat juice and sweetener together. Remove from heat and beat in oil. Combine with dry ingredients and stir until mixture resembles a thick batter that drops with difficulty from a wooden spoon. Add vanilla. (Adjust liquid content accordingly.)

Drop onto oiled cookie sheet. Do not press down. Bake 20–25 minutes or until firm and lightly browned on bottom. Cool on rack.

## Anise Nut Crumbles

3/4 cup concentrated sweetener
2/3 cup safflower oil
1/2 cup roasted ground sunflower seeds
3 cups sifted whole wheat pastry flour
1/2 tsp. sea salt
2 tsp. ground anise

Beat together first two ingredients until creamy and light in texture. Add roasted seeds and beat again.

Sift flour and next two ingredients, and fold into first mixture. Drop onto oiled cookie sheet and bake 25 minutes at 350°F.

## Almond Crumbles

1 cup concentrated sweetener
2/3 cup corn oil
1/2 cup roasted ground almonds
4 cups brown rice flour
1/2 tsp. sea salt
2 tsp. cinnamon
1 tsp. ginger
Hot apple juice

Whisk together first two ingredients until creamy and fluffy. Add roasted ground almonds and beat again.

Sift flour and combine with next three ingredients. Fold into first mixture. Add hot apple juice to make drop consistency.

Preheat oven to 350°F. Drop onto oiled cookie sheet. Bake 25 minutes or until edges are lightly browned.

## Coconut Macaroons

4 egg whites
1/4 tsp. sea salt
1 tsp. lemon juice
1/4 cup concentrated sweetener
1 tsp. lemon rind
1/2 tsp. cinnamon
1 cup roasted ground almonds
1/2 cup coconut
1 tsp. vanilla
1/4–1/2 cup arrowroot flour

Beat whites with sea salt until stiff peaks form. Combine lemon juice and sweetener together. Drip in slowly and keep beating. Fold in rind, cinnamon, almonds, coconut, vanilla and arrowroot. Drop onto oiled paper, or pipe through pastry bag.

Preheat oven to 375°F. Bake 10–15 minutes or until lightly browned and almost firm.

## Jumbles

1/4 cup dried dates
Apple juice or cider to cover dates
1/4 cup oil
1/4 cup concentrated sweetener
1 cup whole wheat pastry flour
1 cup barley flour
1 tsp. anise
1 tsp. cinnamon
1/2 tsp. ginger
1 Tbsp. lemon rind
1/2 tsp. sea salt

3 Tbsp. instant grain coffee
1 tsp. vanilla

Soak dates in juice or cider until soft. Drain and squeeze out moisture. Reserve juice and dice dates.

Combine oil and sweetener. Sift flours, add other dry ingredients and dates. Combine wet mixture with dry mixture, add vanilla and enough reserved juice to form a thick batter that drops with difficulty from a spoon.

Preheat oven to 325°F. Drop batter onto cookie sheet and bake 15–20 minutes or until edges are browned.

**Date Palm** (*Phoenix dactylifera*)
This plant, an important crop of very ancient origin in the Middle East, dates back to at least 3,000 B.C. It grows to a height of about 80 feet. The male and female trees are different, and it is only necessary for the grower to plant one male tree to 50–100 females. Palms may begin to bear fruit about 4 or 5 years after they are planted; but they reach a full bearing age at about 15 years, and continue to bear fruit to about 80 years of age. An average yield for one tree is about 100 lb. of fruit per year.

Dates are grown in desert oases; they are important in the diet of Arab people. There are three kinds of dates: soft dates are eaten raw or used in confectionery; semi-dry dates are sold boxed with the fruits still attached to their strands; dry dates can be preserved for a long period of time. They are quite hard and can even be ground into flour or softened by steeping in water. The chief nutritional value of dates is their high sugar content, which varies from 60 to 70 percent. They also have some vitamin A, $B_1$, $B_2$, and nicotinic acid.

## Orange Cookies

2 cups sultanas
Apple juice or cider
3 cups sweet brown rice flour
1/2 tsp. sea salt
2 Tbsp. orange rind
1-1/4 cup rolled oats
1-1/4 cups roasted crushed sunflower
   seeds
1 tsp. cinnamon
1 tsp. ginger
1/2 cup oil
1/2 cup concentrated sweetener
Juice of two oranges
1 tsp. vanilla

Soak sultanas in juice to cover until soft. Drain, reserve juice, and chop sultanas finely.

Combine next seven ingredients. Beat together oil, sweetener, orange juice and vanilla. Stir into dry mixture, add chopped fruit and reserved juice until mixture drops with difficulty from the end of a wooden spoon.

Preheat oven to 350°F. Oil paper and drop cookies onto paper. Bake 15–20 minutes or until lightly browned.

## Peanut Butter Cookies

1 cup brown rice flour
1 cup rolled barley flakes
1/4 tsp. sea salt
2 tsp. cinnamon
1 tsp. ginger
1 cup chopped raisins
1 cup roasted chopped peanuts
2 tsp. lemon rind
1 cup apple juice
4 Tbsp. peanut butter
1/4 cup oil
1/4 cup concentrated sweetener

Combine first eight ingredients together. Heat next four ingredients, and stir until creamy. Cool and stir into dry mixture.

Preheat oven, drop cookies onto sheet and bake at 350°F for 15–20 minutes or until browned. Cool on rack.

## Poppy Spice

> 1/2 cup sultanas
> Apple juice to cover
> 1 grated apple
> 1 tsp. cinnamon
> 3/4 tsp. ginger
> 1 Tbsp. lemon juice
> 1 Tbsp. lemon rind
> 1/2 cup whole wheat pastry flour
> 1/2 cup corn flour
> 1/4 cup brown rice flour
> 1/2 tsp. sea salt
> 1/2 cup poppy seeds
> 1/3 cup oil

Soak dried fruit in apple juice to cover. Add next five ingredients and stir well. Set aside.

Sift flours and salt together. Drain juice off fruits, and combine with dry mixture.

Roast poppy seeds in dry skillet until they begin to pop. Combine with dry mixture, add oil and enough reserved juice to form a thick batter. Drop onto oiled paper and bake in preheated 375°F oven for 20 minutes or until lightly browned.

### Alternate Method
Combine sultanas, poppy seeds and juice in a heavy saucepan; cook on a medium heat until evaporates and mixture is almost dry. Add 1/2 cup more juice and blend until creamy. Combine with the rest of the ingredients and follow recipe.

## Spice Drops

> 2 cups chopped figs
> Apple juice or cider to cover
> 2 cups whole wheat pastry flour
> 1 cup corn flour
> 1/2 tsp sea salt
> 1 tsp. ginger
> 1/2 tsp. cloves
> 1 tsp. cinnamon
> 1 cup crushed roasted walnuts
> 1/4 cup concentrated sweetener
> 3 eggs
> 1/2 cup oil

Soak figs in juice to cover until soft. Drain and reserve liquid.

Sift next six ingredients together. Add nuts and figs to dry mixture. Set aside.

Combine sweetener and eggs together and beat until light and creamy. Slowly drip in oil and continue beating until oil is absorbed.

Fold 1/3 of egg mixture into dry ingredients, then combine rest of egg mixture with it. Add reserved liquid, if necessary, to form thick batter.

Preheat oven to 350°F and oil cookie sheets. Drop batter from spoon onto sheets. Bake 15–20 minutes or until lightly browned.

## Ginger Drops

> 1-1/2 cups whole wheat pastry flour plus
>   1/4 cup cornmeal
> 1/2 tsp. salt
> 1 tsp. cinnamon
> 1 tsp. ginger powder
> 1/2 tsp. coriander
> 1/4 cup oil
> 1/4 cup concentrated sweetener
> 1 egg

Sift all dry ingredients together. Beat together the last three ingredients until light and creamy. Fold first mixture into wet mixture, and mix only until flour is no longer visible. Drop onto oiled sheet.

Bake in preheated 375°F oven for 10 minutes, then reduce temperature to 350°F and bake 5–10 minutes longer.

# Fruit and Nut Slices

All children love finger things: any sweet or savory food that they can pick up and eat in their hands. Slices have the appeal of both cookies and cakes. They are quick to make, easy to handle and fun to eat.

Slices, because they are usually unleavened, should be baked in rectangular or square baking pans only 1-1/2–2 inches deep; otherwise they will not bake in the center. For parties, try baking them in cupcake or muffin tins. Anyway you serve them, children as well as adults will keep coming back for more. They are a big hit when kids find them in their lunch boxes.

## Basic Fruit Slice

Use any pie, pastry or rolled cookie dough recipe. Divide the dough and roll out on greaseproof paper 1 inch larger than the size of the pan. (Keep other piece of dough covered until ready to use.)

Place dough into oiled pan on bottom only. *Do not stretch.* Bake in preheated 375°F oven for 10 minutes.

Spread any fruit purée over base. Roll out remaining piece of dough the same way. Cover fruit purée with dough, slit dough with knife to allow steam to escape.

Brush with beaten egg yolk and bake at 375°F for 20–25 minutes.

Remove from oven, place on rack; cut slices and cool before removing from pan.

## Bulgur-nut Slice

I created this recipe for one of my first cooking classes. Diana was one of the people in the class who was especially fond of it, perhaps because the bulgur wheat reminded her of her mother's home cooking.

Bulgur wheat has been widely used by the Persians since the fifteenth century B.C. Today, roasted bulgur, and nuts cooked in olive oil make a favorite eggplant stuffing among Middle Eastern people.

> 2 cups Chestnut Purée (p. 64)
> 1 cup raisins or sultanas
> 3–4 cups apple juice or cider
> 1 cup uncooked bulgur
> 1/4 cup oil
> 1/2 tsp. sea salt
> 1 Tbsp. orange or tangerine rind
> 2 cups sweet brown rice flour

Prepare Chestnut Purée. Set aside. (This may be prepared several days in advance.)

Soak raisins or sultanas in apple juice or cider to cover until soft. Reserve liquid. Roast bulgur in oil for a few minutes over medium heat. Add raisins, sea salt and 2 cups boiling apple juice or cider. (Use juice or cider from soaking raisins.) Cover and cook 15–20 minutes on a low heat.

Preheat the oven to 325°F. Oil a small pan and sprinkle it lightly with flour. Combine orange rind and Chestnut Purée. Add the flour to the bulgur, mix in Chestnut Purée and slowly add remaining juice or cider until a thick pancake-like batter is formed. Mix well. Place in pan, cover, and bake 1 hour. Remove cover and bake 15–20 minutes longer or until firm.

### Variation
Add 2 well-beaten eggs to the batter after mixing in Chestnut Purée. Decrease liquid content accordingly. *Do not pat down.* Do not cover while baking.

# Chestnut Brownie

>4-1/2 cups sifted chestnut flour
>2 cups raisins
>Apple juice or cider to cover raisins
>1/4 cup oil
>1/4 tsp. sea salt
>1 tsp. vanilla
>2 cups sifted whole wheat pastry flour
>2 cups chopped roasted walnuts or pine nuts

Dry roast the chestnut flour until it is lightly browned. Set it aside to cool.

Soak the raisins in apple juice or cider to cover until soft. Preheat oven to 325°F; oil a 6×8-inch pan.

Add oil, salt and vanilla to the raisin-juice combination and beat until foamy. Add sifted flours and mix well. The batter should be thick and pancake-like in consistency. (Adjust flour-liquid content accordingly.) Fold in walnuts.

Pour into prepared pan, cover, and bake about 45 minutes. Remove cover and bake 15–20 minutes longer or until cake is set and pulls away from the sides of the pan.

### Variation

Add 1/2 tsp. rosemary to batter. Top each piece with Tofu Cream (p. 147) before serving.

# Christmas Slice

>3 cups raisins or sultanas
>2–3 cups cider
>4 cups chopped apples
>3 cups whole wheat flour
>2 Tbsp. miso
>1/2 cup oil or 1/4 cup sesame butter or tahini
>3 Tbsp. lemon juice
>2 tsp. lemon rind
>2 tsp. vanilla
>1 tsp. cloves
>1 cup roasted chopped walnuts

Combine the raisins or sultanas in a saucepan with enough apple juice or cider to cover. Bring to a boil, cover, and simmer about 30 minutes. Roast the flour in a dry skillet until it begins to brown lightly. Set aside to cool. Cut the apples into small pieces (peel if not organic), toss together with flour.

Preheat the oven to 325°F; oil and lightly flour the baking pan.

Dissolve the miso in a small amount of the warm juice from the boiled raisins. Combine the next six ingredients. (You may boil raisins with a vanilla bean and omit the liquid vanilla.) Add this mixture to the flour-apple combination, folding in until a thick batter has formed.

Spoon into pan, cover and bake 40 minutes. Remove cover and bake about 20 minutes longer or until slice pulls away from the sides of the pan. Remove from the oven and place on a rack to cool.

# Ginger by the Sea

Every summer, Joanne and her family go to their summer home in Nantascet, Massachusetts. Joanne not only cooks and bakes for her husband and five children, but for a constant stream of friends that visit her open house daily. This is one of the many delightful treats that she serves.

>1 cup raisins or sultanas
>2 cups corn flour
>2 cups whole wheat pastry flour
>1 tsp. sea salt
>1 tsp. ginger
>1/2 cup oil
>1 egg yolk
>3/4 cup maple syrup
>1/4–1/2 cup liquid
>APPLE TOPPING:
>2 cups applesauce
>1 egg white
>1 pinch of sea salt

Soak the raisins or sultanas in liquid to cover until soft. Dry roast the flours separately until brown. Set aside to cool. Preheat the oven to 350°F.

Combine first five ingredients. In a separate bowl, beat together oil, yolk, and maple syrup until thick and creamy. Fold first mixture into oil and syrup.

Oil and lightly flour a baking pan. Spoon batter into the pan. Cover pan and bake 45 minutes. Remove the cover and bake 15–20 minutes longer, or until firm.

Prepare applesauce. Beat egg white and sea salt until peaked. Fold egg white into sauce.

During the last 5 minutes of baking, place topping on cake and bake at 400°F.

**Ginger** (*Zingiber officinale*)
Ginger is a tropical plant, native to Asia, where it has been cultivated since ancient times. The roots, or *rhizomes*, are dug up when the plant is about 10 months old.

The Chinese traditionally use ginger as an external remedy for cataracts, to cure dyspepsia, or settle a nauseous stomach; it is also used as a tonic to strengthen the heart, and as a sedative.

Dried ginger is made by a complicated process of washing, soaking or boiling, peeling and drying. Fresh, unprocessed ginger is also available.

Ginger is grown throughout the tropics for local consumption, and is exported from West Africa, Jamaica and India. It is widely used all over the world for its pungent flavor, and is a major ingredient in curry powders. Ginger root or powder is also used in making ginger beer and gingerbread. Dried ginger is very concentrated and should be used sparingly in all baking.

## Walnut-ginger Slice

  1/4 cup bulgur or couscous
  4 Tbsp. oil
  1 cup raisins
  2 tsp. cinnamon
  1 Tbsp. ginger
  1/2 tsp. sea salt
  1/2 tsp. cloves
  3–4 cups boiling apple juice or cider
  2 cups grated carrots
  1/2 cup whole wheat pastry flour
  1 cup corn flour
  1/2 cup oil or 1/4 cup tahini
  1-1/2 cups roasted chopped walnuts
  APPLE SAUCE TOPPING:
  8–9 medium-sized apples
  1 tsp. cinnamon
  1/2 tsp. cloves
  1/2 tsp. ginger
  1/2 tsp. sea salt
  2 tsp. lemon juice
  1/2 cup raisins

Sauté bulgur in 2 Tbsp. oil. Add raisins, cinnamon, ginger, sea salt, cloves and 3 cups boiling apple juice or cider; cover and cook for 10 minutes. Sauté carrots in 2 Tbsp. oil. Combine grated carrots and cooked bulgur. Fold flour and oil into the mixture.

Preheat the oven to 350°F; oil and lightly flour a rectangular baking pan.

Add the nuts and more apple juice or cider until the batter has a heavy pancake-like consistency, thick enough to drop with difficulty from a wooden spoon.

Pour batter into pan. Cover and bake about 45 minutes; uncover and bake 15 minutes longer or until slice pulls away from the sides of pan. Remove from the oven and cool on a cake rack.

*Topping*
Core and slice apples. (Peel if not organic.) Place apples, spices, sea salt and lemon juice in a pot. Cover and cook until apples are soft. Blend sauce in a food mill or blender.

(If using a blender, set at a very low speed for a very short time.) Add raisins and cool.

If desired, add arrowroot diluted in 2 Tbsp. apple juice or cider to sauce after blending and return to heat. Cook, constantly stirring, until mixture begins to thicken and boil. Use 1 Tbsp. arrowroot per cup of applesauce.

### Couscous Variation

Substitute 1 cup couscous for bulgur. Sauté couscous in 1/4 cup oil. Combine raisins, cinnamon, sea salt, cloves, and 2 cups warm juice or cider with couscous mixture. Set aside for 30 minutes. Combine this mixture with 2 cups more juice or cider and bring to a boil. Add the rest of ingredients and proceed as in recipe.

## Layered Almond Slice

BASE:
2 cups whole wheat pastry flour
1/4 tsp. sea salt
1/3 cup oil
Apple juice to form dough

FIRST TOPPING:
2 eggs
2 Tbsp. concentrated sweetener
1/4 tsp. sea salt
1-1/2 tsp. vanilla
2 cups chopped almonds

SECOND TOPPING:
4 Tbsp. tahini
1-1/2 cups apple juice
2 Tbsp. concentrated sweetener
2 Tbsp. instant grain coffee
1/2 bar agar-agar

*Base*

Place flour and salt in a mixing bowl. Add oil, cutting it in until it looks like bread crumbs. Preheat oven to 375°F and oil rectangular baking pan.

Add enough liquid to mixture to form a dough. Roll out on oiled greaseproof paper and place in baking pan. Prick base with fork and bake 10 minutes.

*First topping*

Beat eggs, sweetener, salt and vanilla. Add chopped nuts. Remove crust from oven, spread egg mixture over it and bake 10 minutes or until set. Cool.

*Second topping*

Blend tahini, juice, sweetener, coffee together. Shred in agar-agar and bring to a boil. Lower heat and simmer 5 minutes.

Pour mixture on first layer and sprinkle with ground almonds. Cool and set. Cut into bars when cold.

## Spice Slice

2 cups raisins
Apple juice or cider to cover raisins
1 cup couscous
1 cup roasted brown rice flour
2 cups whole wheat pastry flour
1 tsp. cinnamon
1/2 tsp. cloves
2 tsp. orange, tangerine or lemon rind
1/2 tsp. sea salt
1/2 cup oil
3 cups diced apples

Soak raisins in juice or cider until soft. Reserve liquid.

Combine all dry ingredients. Add oil to dry mixture, rubbing with your hands until oil is fully absorbed.

Dice apples. (Peel if not organic.) Boil reserved juice. Add apples and raisins to the dry mixture and slowly pour boiled juice or cider over the mixture until the consistency is pancake-like—thick enough to drop from a wooden spoon. Add more boiled liquid if necessary.

Pour batter into pan, cover and bake in a preheated 350°F oven for 1 hour. Remove cover and bake 15–20 minutes longer or until slice is set and lightly browned.

## Sunshine Coconut Slice

1-1/2 cups corn flour
1-1/2 cups brown rice flour
1/2 cup whole wheat pastry flour
1/2 tsp. sea salt
1/2 cup oil
Apple juice or cider
2–3 cups date and raisin purée (p. 64)
2 cups coconut

Dry roast each flour separately until lightly browned. Cool and combine with sea salt.

Rub in oil until mixture resembles tiny bread crumbs. Add just enough apple juice to moisten mixture.

Preheat oven to 350°F. Oil baking pan and sprinkle crumb mixture onto bottom. Press down.

Prebake 5 minutes. Cover with a layer of fruit purée. Bake 10–15 minutes or until fruit is almost dry. Sprinkle on coconut and bake another 5 minutes. Cool, and cut into slices.

**Walnut** (*Juglans regia*)
The walnut tree is valuable not only for its fruit, but also for its timber. Oil is extracted from the nuts and is important for its edible qualities, as well as being a preparation used in paints for artists. The walnut grows up to 100 feet high, with green fruit sometimes picked before it hardens, and eaten pickled in vinegar. If allowed to harden, the fruit is then picked and used as nuts for dessert making and baking.

## Walnut Slice

3 eggs
1/2 cup concentrated sweetener
1/2 cup oil
3 cups sifted whole wheat pastry flour
1 tsp. cinnamon
1/2 tsp. cloves
2 tsp. orange rind
1 tsp. lemon rind
2 cups chopped walnuts
1/2 tsp. sea salt
1 tsp. vanilla
Juice and rind of 1 orange
Apple juice to form thick batter

Combine eggs and sweetener together, and beat until creamy and light. Slowly drip in oil and continue beating until absorbed. Set aside.

Sift flour, and combine with next six ingredients. Mix vanilla, orange juice and rind together, add to egg mixture. Combine wet mixture with dry mixture.

Stir until thick batter is formed. (Adjust liquid content accordingly.)

Preheat oven to 375°F and oil baking pan. Spoon into pan, and bake 25–35 minutes or until slice pulls away from the sides of the pan. Test by inserting a skewer into the center of the slice. If it comes out clean, slice is done.

## *Azuki*-bean Slice

1 cup dried chestnuts
1 cup uncooked *azuki* beans*
Apple juice or cider to cover
1 cup raisins
4 cups apple juice or cider
1/2 tsp. sea salt
1/2 cup roasted chopped walnuts

---

*Azuki* beans are very small red beans which can be found in most natural food shops, Chinese, Korean or Japanese stores.

1/4 cup chestnut or whole wheat flour
1-1/4 tsp. vanilla

Soak chestnuts and *azuki* beans overnight in apple juice or cider to cover. Reserve liquid. Pressure-cook beans, chestnuts and 1/2 cup raisins together in 4 cups liquid (from soaking chestnuts) for 30 minutes. Add sea salt and simmer 30 minutes longer on a low heat. Toss 1/2 cup raisins and nuts lightly in flour and set aside. Oil a rectangular pan. Preheat the oven to 375°F.

Purée half of the cooked mixture in a food mill or blender. Combine all mixtures and add vanilla. (Adjust liquid-flour content to form a heavy thick mixture.) Spread into pan. Bake 45 minutes or until firm.

## Applesauce Slice

> 2 cups applesauce
> 1/2 cup concentrated sweetener
> 1/2 cup oil
> 1/2 cup raisins
> 1/2 cup roasted chopped walnuts or
>    sunflower seeds
> 4 cups sifted whole wheat pastry flour
> 2 tsp. cinnamon
> 3/4 tsp. cloves
> 2 tsp. ginger
> 1 tsp. sea salt

Whisk together applesauce and sweetener. Slowly drip in the oil, beating continuously. Preheat the oven to 350°F. Oil baking pan. Toss raisins and nuts with a small amount of the flour.

Sift the remaining ingredients, add to the applesauce mixture, and stir until batter is smooth and creamy. Fold in raisins and nuts. The consistency should be thick and pancake-like. Adjust flour-liquid content accordingly.

Pour into baking pan and bake 40–50

minutes, or until slice pulls away from the sides of the pan and is springy to the touch.

## O'George Bars

While baking for stores and restaurants in New York City, Sara and I discovered this recipe. We sold these bars on our push-cart which we wheeled around Central Park in the summertime. It was our most popular item.

> 4 cups sweet brown rice flour
> 1 cup rolled oats
> 1-1/2 cups sesame seeds
> 2 tsp. cinnamon
> 1 Tbsp. orange rind
> 1/2 tsp. sea salt
> 2 cups raisins
> 3 cups roasted crushed nuts
> 1/2 cup peanut butter
> 1 cup apple juice or cider
> 1 tsp. vanilla
> 1/4 cup hot concentrated sweetener

Combine all dry ingredients. Blend peanut butter, 1/2 cup juice, vanilla and concentrated sweetener until smooth and creamy. Combine dry mixture with liquid mixture, adding more juice if necessary to form a thick batter.

Preheat oven to 350°F and oil baking pan. Spoon batter into pan, cover, and bake 45 minutes. Remove cover and bake until firm. Cool on rack and brush with sweetener to add a glaze on top.

### Variations
1. Substitute any nut butter for peanut and any nuts for peanuts.
2. Substitute seeds for peanuts.
3. Use any dried fruit.
4. Substitute 2 cups couscous for 2 cups flour.

# 8. SUMMER FUN: Cooling Desserts

## Ice Cream Story

When Nero was emperor of Rome, one of his favorite desserts was created by adding honey and fruit juice to snow. This was probably the first form of sherbet recorded in history. Eventually, a recipe was brought out of China whereby milk was substituted for snow, but since it had to be frozen, only a handful of people could enjoy it.

What is the ice cream like today that we are all eating too much of? Americans consume more than 700 million gallons a year, which means that the average American will consume 16 quarts per person. In the good old days, when ice cream was made of whole eggs, milk and sugar with natural flavoring added, it was a rare treat which the family tediously cranked together and shared maybe once a week. Today, most ice creams are synthetic from start to finish. Here is a little example of what you may expect to find in some of them:

1. *Ethyl acetate*—used to give a pineapple flavor. It is used as a cleaner for textiles and leather goods, highly toxic vapors

have been known to cause chronic liver, lung and heart damage.

2. *Amyl acetate*—used for banana flavoring and paint solvent.
3. *Diethylen glucol*—a chemical used as an emulsifier in addition to or in place of eggs. It is the chemical that is used in anti-freeze and paint removers.
4. *Benzyl acetate*—used for strawberry flavoring and as a nitrate solvent.
5. *Butyraldehyde*—used for its nut flavoring abilities. It's also used to make rubber cement.

So, now you may be looking at the ice cream you eat with different eyes. Be discriminating, and if you can't find any "real" ice cream, try making some of your own desserts. These will easily fill the gap. Try the following parfait, cream, custard, and ice cream recipes to satisfy those hungry little mouths.

# Forget Me Knots

1. Cold desserts can be frozen if they contain agar-agar.
2. When freezing desserts in refrigerator trays, they should be frozen to a fairly solid consistency, beaten until fluffy and then quickly returned to the freezer to freeze again. This is the best method for ice cream.
3. To convert your favorite recipes, instead of cow's or goat's milk, use soy milk, or any nut milk, as the base.
4. French Ice Cream uses egg yolks to obtain it's richness in addition to cream, sugar, salt and flavoring—6 yolks to 4 cups cream.
5. Italian Ice Cream uses both yolks and whites beaten separately, folding in whites at the end, before freezing.

# Recipes

## Ice Cream

### Vanilla Ice Cream

1 bar agar-agar
1 cup apple juice
1 cup blanched almonds
2 cups hot apple juice or soy milk
1/2 cup concentrated sweetener
1/2 tsp. sea salt
1 tsp. cinnamon
1 tsp. dried mint
1 Tbsp. vanilla
1/4 cup oil

Wash and shred agar-agar into apple juice. Bring to a boil, cover and simmer 5 minutes.

Blend together juice and almonds until creamy. Add the rest of the ingredients except oil. Slowly drip in oil as you beat or blend. Add agar-agar mixture and whip until creamy.

Place in freezer until frozen, whip and freeze again.

You may also just serve this without freezing. Quite refreshing!

### Strawberry Ice Cream

1 cup apple juice
1 bar agar-agar
1 cup hot apple juice
2/3 cup cashews
1/2 cup date purée (p. 64)
2 Tbsp. carob
1 Tbsp. miso or 1/2 tsp. sea salt
1 tsp. ginger
1 Tbsp. lemon rind
2 tsp. vanilla
1/2 cup strawberries

Shred agar-agar into apple juice. Bring to a boil. Lower heat, cover and simmer 5 minutes. Set aside.

Prepare date purée and combine with all the rest of the ingredients, blending until smooth and creamy. (Reserve some of the strawberries for topping.)

Whip in agar-agar mixture and blend again quickly.

This dessert can now be served as is, or frozen, beaten and frozen again.

*Ice Cream Flavors*

1. Add 3–4 Tbsp. carob powder to any ice cream recipe and cook with agar-agar mixture.
2. Add 1 cup coconut while blending.
3. Substitute 1 cup fresh fruit in season for 1 cup apple juice.
4. Substitute 1/2 cup nut butter for 1 cup nuts.

**Strawberry** (*Fragariaan ananassa*)
The strawberry is a plant native to North America. Growing mostly in the woodlands of the eastern part of the United States, it radiates stems or runners which take root and grow into new plants. It has a thick, dark foliage, and bears white or pinkish flowers. Male and female flowers are born on separate plants; female plants will not flower into fruit unless planted with males. Used mainly as a dessert fruit, strawberries can also be made into jam, used in pies, cakes and tarts.

# Custards

## Orange Custard

> 2 Tbsp. whole wheat pastry, corn or
>   chestnut flour
> 1/4 cup concentrated sweetener
> Juice and grated rind of 1 orange
> 1 egg
> 1 tsp. lemon juice
> 1/4 tsp. sea salt

Roast flour in oil until lightly browned. Set aside to cool.

Combine flour and sweetener together. Add juice and rind, and cook in a heavy saucepan over a medium heat, stirring constantly until mixture boils.

Beat eggs slightly. Add lemon juice and sea salt. Combine this with the flour mixture, and cook 5 minutes on a low heat, stirring constantly so that egg does not overcook.

## Strawberry Tahini Custard

> 1-1/2 bars agar-agar
> 3 cups cider or juice
> 1 cup apple juice or water
> 2 Tbsp. tahini
> 2 cups chopped strawberries
> 3 Tbsp. arrowroot
> 1 Tbsp. vanilla

Rinse agar-agar under cold running water. Squeeze out excess liquid. Shred into 2 cups juice or cider. Bring to a boil on a medium heat. Lower heat and cook until agar-agar dissolves. Blend 1 cup liquid and tahini until creamy. Add to agar-agar mixture. Stir in strawberries. Dissolve arrowroot in remaining 1 cup juice and add to custard. Stir until mixture boils. Remove from heat, add vanilla and cool.

## Lemon Custard

> 2-1/2 Tbsp. whole wheat pastry flour
> 1 Tbsp. oil
> 1 egg
> 2 cups apple juice or cider
> 4 Tbsp. lemon juice
> 4 Tbsp. lemon rind
> 1/4 tsp. sea salt

Roast flour in oil until lightly browned. Set aside to cool.

Separate egg. Stir yolk with a fork. Combine flour with a few Tbsp. apple juice and stir into a smooth and creamy batter. Remove all lumps. Combine with egg yolk and remaining juice. Cook in a double boiler, stirring constantly for 5 minutes.

Beat egg white and sea salt together until peaked. Add lemon juice, rind, and egg white to the cooked mixture. Fold in gently. *Do not overmix.*

**Variations**
Add any one or a combination of the following:

> 2 to 3 Tbsp. instant grain coffee, before
>   cooking
> Mint to taste, before or after cooking
> 1 tsp. cinnamon, after cooking
> 1/4 cup crushed roasted nuts or seeds
>   before folding in egg white
> 1/2 cup fresh diced fruit to yolk mixture, after cooking
> Also see variations for Oat Cream
>   (p. 145)

# Creams

## Chestnut Cream I

> 2 cups cooked chestnuts (1 cup dried)
> 1/2–1 cup apple juice
> 3–4 Tbsp. tahini

2 Tbsp. concentrated sweetener
1/4 tsp. sea salt
1 tsp. cinnamon
1 tsp. vanilla

Soak chestnuts overnight for quicker cooking. Bring to a boil and simmer covered until tender.

If pressure-cooking, pressure 45 minutes in enough liquid to cover.

Drain off liquid from chestnuts and reserve.

While they are still hot, blend the chestnuts together with the next six ingredients. (If you want a thinner consistency, thin with warm apple juice.)

If you blend or cream the chestnuts when they get cold, it will be almost impossible to get a good creamy consistency because of their high fat content.

**Cinnamon** (*Cinnamomum zeylanicum*)
Cinnamon is mainly used as a spice in flavoring desserts such as pies, cookies, cakes, custards and pastries. It came originally from South India and Ceylon, and is cultivated only in warm tropical climates.

Planted as a seed, after 2 years it is ready to be harvested. The bark is removed in strips. The outer skin of the bark is scraped off, and the strips are dried very slowly. They are pale brown in color and as they dry they curl into each other forming what we know as "cinnamon sticks." There are many different grades of cinnamon, the quality depending on where it is grown and the various colors, ranging from light to dark brown.

# Chestnut Cream II

1 recipe Chestnut Cream I
1 bar agar-agar
2 cups apple juice

Rinse agar-agar under cold running water quickly. Squeeze out excess liquid.

Shread into juice, and bring to a boil. Lower heat, cover and simmer 5 minutes. Blend together with Chestnut Cream I.

This mixture will set when cold. It can be used for various desserts, such as pies, or ice cream. For ice cream you would have to freeze, whip and freeze again for best results.

# Oat Cream

1 cup rolled oats
4–6 cups apple juice or cider
1/4 cup tahini
1/2 tsp. sea salt
1/4 cup concentrated sweetener
1 tsp. cinnamon
1 tsp. vanilla

Roast oats until lightly browned. Combine juice, tahini and oats in a heavy pot. Add sea salt and sweetener, and bring to a boil, stirring occasionally. Lower heat, cover and simmer at least 20 minutes.

After cooking, add cinnamon and vanilla. Blend until creamy and smooth. Adjust liquid content until desired texture is attained. This can be kept under refrigeration for several weeks.

## Variations
1. Add 4 Tbsp. grain coffee substitute before cooking.
2. Add 1 tsp. cinnamon, 1/2 tsp. ginger and 1 tsp. orange, tangerine or lemon rind after cooking.
3. Add 2 tsp. mint before cooking.
4. Add the juice and grated rind of 1

orange, tangerine or lemon after cooking.

5. Add 1/2 cup cooked chestnuts (p. 144) to cream after cooking, and before or after blending.
6. Add 1/2 cup chopped, roasted nuts or seeds after blending.
7. Add 1 to 2 tsp. more vanilla after cooking, or vanilla bean before cooking.
8. Substitute 1/2–1 cup apple butter or apple cider jelly for 1/2 cup juice.
9. Substitute mu tea, or mint tea for juice, and add 1/2 cup concentrated sweetener before or after cooking.
10. Substitute whole wheat pastry flour, chestnut or corn flour for oats.

### Almond (*Rosaceae*)

Almonds are one of the fruits of the rose family. Originally, the almond is thought to have come from one of the Mediterranean countries, where it is still widely grown. Nearly all of the almonds grown in the United States are produced in California.

The tree is medium-size, related to the peach and grown chiefly for its nuts. The beautiful pinkish-white blossoms open in early spring before the long, pointed leaves appear. The edible seed or nut is enclosed within a small dry shell.

Almonds contain a large percentage of oil, and are also made into almond butter, used in baking and cooking. There are two kinds of almonds: sweet and bitter. Sweet almonds, a popular delicacy, are eaten roasted or salted, or are used in the cooking and baking of pastries.

The bitter almond is a variety of the common almond, but is usually not considered edible. Because of the large quantity of hydrocyanic acid it contains, the oil is most frequently used in medicines, or as a flavoring extract (almond extract) for baking, after the acid has been removed.

## Almond Cream

1 cup almonds
Apple juice or cider
2 eggs
2 Tbsp. almond butter
1 Tbsp. lemon juice
Rind of 1/4 lemon
1/4 tsp. sea salt

Blend almonds and cream* with a little apple juice until smooth. Beat eggs, warm almond butter and add to egg mixture. Combine the rest of the ingredients and cook in a double boiler till thick.

## Pastry Cream

3 Tbsp. whole wheat pastry flour
1–2 cups apple juice or cider
1–2 Tbsp. concentrated sweetener
3 egg yolks
1/4 tsp. sea salt
1/2 tsp. orange rind
1 Tbsp. oil
1/2 tsp. vanilla

Roast flour until lightly browned. Set aside to cool. Heat apple juice in top of double boiler or heavy saucepan. Remove from pan or boiler. Cool. Place sweetener, yolks, flour, sea salt and rind in double boiler. Pour apple juice slowly into the sweetener mixture, beating with rotary beater or wire whisk. Do not boil.

Cook until thickened, stirring occasionally. Remove from heat, add oil and vanilla, mix well.

See variations for Oat Cream (p. 145).

---

* Use a *suribachi* or blender for best results.

## Instant Tofu Cream

    2 cups tofu (p. 24)
    1/2 cup date purée (p. 64)
    3 Tbsp. tahini, or almond butter
    1 tsp. vanilla
    1/4 tsp. sea salt

Drop tofu into boiling salted water. Remove from heat. Combine with remaining ingredients, blending until creamy. Add fruit juice if difficult to blend.

## Tofu Cream

    1/2 cup apple juice or cider
    2 Tbsp. tahini, almond butter
    2 cups tofu
    1/4 tsp. sea salt
    1-1/2 Tbsp. arrowroot flour
    1/4 cup concentrated sweetener
    3 Tbsp. apple cider or juice
    1 tsp. vanilla

Bring apple juice to a boil. Blend with next three ingredients until creamy. Dilute arrowroot in sweetener and apple juice or cider.

    Place tofu mixture in pan, and when almost boiling, add arrowroot mixture, stirring rapidly until mixture boils and thickens. Remove from heat. Stir in vanilla.

    See Oat Cream variations (p. 145).

## Tofu Whip Cream

    1 cup tofu
    2–3 Tbsp. concentrated sweetener
    1 Tbsp. oil or nut butter
    Pinch of sea salt
    1/2 bar agar-agar
    1/2 cup apple juice or cider
    1 tsp. vanilla

Drop tofu into boiling salted water. Remove from heat and let sit 2–3 minutes. Squeeze out liquid.

    Blend tofu, sweetener, oil or nut butter and sea salt together until creamy. Set aside.

    Rinse the agar-agar under cold running water. Squeeze out excess liquid and shred into small pieces. Pour liquid over agar-agar and bring to a boil; lower heat and simmer until agar-agar dissolves. Stir occasionally. Remove from heat.

    Add vanilla and tofu cream mixture. Beat with wire whisk or electric mixer until smooth and creamy. Set aside to jell. When the mixture has almost set, beat again. Set aside for a few hours to mellow.

    Chill if not using immediately. To freshen, beat again before using.

    See variations for Oat Cream (p. 145)

## Tofu Sour Cream I

    1 cup tofu
    Juice of 1 lemon (2–3 Tbsp.)
    1/2–1 tsp. sea salt

Drop tofu into boiling salted water. Drain and discard cooking water.

    Place tofu in a blender, add lemon juice and salt. Blend until creamy and taste. If it is too sour, add more salt or hot water to counteract lemon.

## Tofu Sour Cream II

    1/2 tsp. cinnamon
    1/2–1 tsp. vanilla
    1 cup Tofu Sour Cream I
    1/2 diced apple (peel if not organic)
    1/4 cup raisins

Blend cinnamon and vanilla with Tofu Sour Cream I; add fruit and mix together. Use as a filling or cake topping.

**Variations**

1. Use any fresh fruit in season in place of apples.
2. Use any dried fruit; soak and dice.
3. Add roasted chopped nuts or seeds, before or after blending.
4. Add 1 to 2 tsp. concentrated sweetener and 1 tsp. lemon juice to fruit.
5. Allow to marinate for several hours before mixing with cream.
6. Also see Oat Cream variations (p. 145).

# Parfaits

Basically, a parfait is a mixture of beaten eggs or egg whites into which hot, cooked syrup is mixed. Whipped cream and fruits are usually folded in and can be frozen in a mold or refrigerated until served. However, some people have asked me how to make a cooling, refreshing summer dessert without eggs. So for those who do not wish to use eggs, here are a few suggestions:

## Black and White Parfait

2 bars agar-agar
6 cups apple juice
3 Tbsp. tahini
2 Tbsp. grain coffee
Pinch of sea salt
Applesauce or dried fruit purée for in between layers
Mint for garnish

Rinse agar-agar under cold water rather quickly. Squeeze out excess liquid and shred each bar into 3 cups juice and salt.

In two separate saucepans, bring each mixture to a boil, lower heat, cover and simmer 5 minutes. Put instant grain coffee into blender, add 3 cups boiled juice-agar-agar combination, 1-1/2 Tbsp. tahini and whip until creamy.

Repeat with other juice-agar-agar mixture, adding 1-1/2 Tbsp. tahini and whip until creamy and smooth. Cool in separate bowls until firm. Blend each one separately, pour into rinsed parfait glasses, alternating layers—black and white—placing fruit layer in between. Top with fresh mint.

## Carob Parfait

2 cups apple juice
1 cup dates
1/2 lb. tofu
3/4 cup lightly roasted cashews
3 Tbsp. carob
1 Tbsp. orange rind
1/2 tsp. sea salt
1 tsp. vanilla

Cook together apple juice and dates until they are soft. Drop tofu into boiling water, bring to a boil and drain. Blend together with juice, dates, and roasted cashews until creamy. Add the rest of the ingredients. Blend again until smooth and light in texture.

Place in parfait glasses alternating with fresh or dried fruit. Serve chilled.

## Peach Parfait

3 peaches
2 bars agar-agar
5 cups apple juice or cider
4 Tbsp. arrowroot flour
4 Tbsp. apple juice or cider or 2 Tbsp. concentrated sweetener and 2 Tbsp. juice
1/4 tsp. sea salt
2 tsp. lemon juice
1/2 cup roasted chopped nuts

1 cup blueberries or strawberries

Slice the peaches into thin vertical strips. (If not organic, blanch them, p. 16.) Rinse the agar-agar under cold running water. Squeeze out the excess liquid. Shred into small pieces and combine it with the 5 cups cider. Cook the cider and agar-agar together until liquid comes to a boil. Lower heat and cook until agar-agar dissolves.

Dilute arrowroot in 4 Tbsp. juice or juice-sweetener combination. Add this to agar-agar mixture and bring to a boil, stirring constantly. Then quickly add peaches, sea salt, lemon juice and nuts. Bring to a boil, stirring rapidly. Cook until mixture turns clearer and thickens. Alternately spoon the mixture and berries into parfait glasses. Allow to cool at room temperatue, or chill until set.

## Almond Parfait

4 eggs plus 1/4 tsp. sea salt
2 cups Almond Whip Cream*
1 cup concentrated sweetener

Add sea salt to eggs and beat until yolks and whites are well blended. Heat sweetener to boiling, lower heat and simmer 3–4 minutes. Pour in a steady stream into eggs, beating constantly. Cook in a double boiler until thick, stirring continuously. Cool. Prepare Almond Whip Cream.

Fold almond cream into first mixture. Fill glasses alternating with fruit purée or cooked fresh fruit. Refrigerate or freeze until serving.

**Peach** (*Prunus persica*)
The tree from which the peach originates is a small, deciduous type, producing small pink and sometimes white flowers from which spring forth peaches varying from greenish white to yellow. Peaches mostly grow in countries with warm climate like the United States, China, Japan, South Africa and Australia.

---

* *Almond whip cream:* Blanch 2 cups almonds in boiling water to remove skins. Roast in oven until dry and lightly browned. Blend with warm apple juice and vanilla until thick and creamy. (It should drop with reluctance from the edge of a wooden spoon.)

# 9. LITTLE NIBBLES: *No Bake Candy Treats*

There will always be those times when you feel like a "little nibble" and would give your weight in gold if there was a snack within reach. The following recipe ideas are intended to stimulate your creativity and whet your appetite. This section is filled with natural treats that can be used for a quick treat for anyone in the family or when the unexpected guest drops in. However, don't get stuck in this chapter which is easy to do because they are quite delicious indeed!

## Forget Me Knots

1. The amount of liquid necessary for each recipe will differ each time, according to the moisture in the ingredients (especially *nut butters*), humidity in the room, water content in the sweetener, and how finely you are able to grind your seeds and nuts.

2. Use all ingredients at room temperature, unless otherwise instructed.
3. Try to obtain dried fruits without sulphur dioxide or sorbic acid.*
4. Choose concentrated sweetener according to the consistency of the recipe you are preparing as well as the taste.
5. Allow candies to harden before serving.

# Recipes

**Peanut** (*Arachis hypogaea*)
The peanut is an annual herb of the pea family, its fruit being a pod and not a nut. Peanuts are native to South America; the Indians were growing peanuts there at least 1000 years ago. Today, they are grown in semi-arid regions as well as in other parts of the world and have the ability to endure long drought and grow when the rain comes.

The peanut contains pound for pound more protein than sirloin steak, more carbohydrates than potatoes, and one third as much fat as butter.

Peanut hulls have the food value of course hay, and the thin skin that covers the nut is sometimes used in place of wheat bran in cattle fodder. Also the roots of the plant, if left in the soil, enrich it with valuable nitrogen products.

## Peanut Popcorn

4 Tbsp. oil
1/2 cup unpopped popcorn
1/2 tsp. sea salt
1-1/2 cup chopped almonds
1/2 cup concentrated sweetener
1/2 cup barley malt or maltose
1 tsp. vanilla
1/2 cup peanut butter

Heat oil in heavy pot. Add corn and salt. Place lid on pot allowing a little crack so that excess steam can escape. Cook over high heat, turning pot around until all corn is popped.

In a large pan combine popcorn and almonds; keep warm in a 250°F oven. Oil the side of a heavy saucepan, combine sweetener and malt. Bring to a boil. Stir continuously for 5 minutes or until mixture reaches the soft ball stage on a candy thermometer. Remove from heat, stir in peanut butter and vanilla till creamy. Immediately pour over popcorn mixture, stirring to coat. Cool, and break into bite-size pieces.

## Sprouted Wheat Balls

1-1/4 cups sprouted wheat
2-1/4 cups pitted dates
1/4 cup currants
1 cup minced walnuts or almonds
1/2 cup roasted sesame seeds
1/2 Tbsp. miso
1/4 cup concentrated sweetener
2 Tbsp. peanut butter
1-1/2 Tbsp. lemon rind
1 tsp. coriander

Grind first two ingredients together. Add the rest of the ingredients, slowly working them

---

\* Sulphur dioxide is used as a preservative in dried fruit to prevent browning and oxidation of fruit, mold growth and loss of vitamin C after drying.

Sorbic acid is used as a preservative in dried tree fruit.

into fruit mix. Form into balls and press half an almond in the center of each ball. Roll in coconut if desired.

## Sprouted Wheat Candy

2 cups sprouted wheat
2 cups pitted dates or chopped figs
1/2 cup dried apricots
1/2 cup coconut
1 cup roasted cashews
1/2 cup almond butter
1-1/2 Tbsp. orange rind
1/2 Tbsp. lemon rind
1 Tbsp. cinnamon
1 tsp. vanilla
1/2 tsp. sea salt

Blend or grind first four ingredients together. Mix in the rest of the ingredients and beat until too stiff to mix. Shape into logs, wrap in greaseproof paper and chill.

## Carob Candy

1 cup concentrated sweetener
1/2 cup carob powder
1 cup ground roasted hazelnuts
1/2 cup chopped roasted almonds
1/2 cup coconut
1/2 cup ground roasted sunflower seeds
1/2 Tbsp. miso
1 tsp. coriander or cinnamon
1 tsp. vanilla

Combine all ingredients, mixing well. Oil pan and spread out 1/2 inch thick. Set in refrigerator to harden.

## Nut Balls

1 cup peanut butter
1 cup concentrated sweetener
2 cups roasted sesame seeds
4 Tbsp. coconut
1 tsp. cinnamon
1/4 tsp. sea salt

Mix all ingredients together in an oiled bowl. Shape into little balls and roll in additional coconut before serving.

**Coconut**

Coconuts, the fruit of the coconut palm (*cocos nucifera*), grow in large clusters among giant, feather-like leaves. About twelve new leaves appear each year, and an equal number of compound flower stalks push out from the base of the older leaves. Thirty female flowers, and ten thousand male flowers appear on each stalk, maturing at different times, thereby assuring cross-pollination. Flowering begins when the tree is about five years old, and continues thereafter.

Each coconut has a smooth, light colored rind, under which is found a 1 or 2-inch-thick tough husk of brownish-red fibers. The rind and husk surround a brown woody shell that has three soft spots or "eyes" at one end. The rind and husk are usually discarded before the coconuts are shipped to market.

The coconut seed lies inside the shell in the shape of a crisp white ball of coconut meat, surrounded by a tough, brown skin. Its hollow center contains a sugary liquid referred to as coconut "milk." The coconut seed is one of the largest of all seeds, measuring 8 to 12 inches long and 6 to 10 inches across. It requires about one year to ripen.

Coconut fruits float easily and have been dispersed widely by ocean currents throughout the tropics. The native home of the coconut palm is unknown. They flourish best close to the sea on low-lying areas a few feet above water where there is circulating ground water and ample rainfall.

Most of the world's coconuts are produced in the Philippines, Indonesia, India, Ceylon and Malaysia.

## Carob Logs

1/4 cup maple syrup
1/2 cup tahini
1/2 cup carob powder
1/2 cup roasted ground cashews
1/2 cup roasted ground almonds
1/2 cup finely chopped dates or figs
1/2 Tbsp. miso
1 tsp. coriander
1 tsp. cinnamon
1 Tbsp. lemon rind

Combine maple syrup and tahini in a heavy saucepan, and cook over a low heat until melted. Remove from heat and immediately stir in the rest of the ingredients. Shape into logs and set aside to rest for at least 1 hour. Roll in coconut if desired, or top with carob glaze recipe that follows.

## Carob Cover

1/2 cup concentrated sweetener
1/2 cup carob powder
1/4 cup tahini
1/4 tsp. sea salt
2 tsp. vanilla

Heat sweetener in heavy saucepan until warm. Stir in carob powder (sift if lumpy) and continue to cook, stirring constantly until just under boiling. Stir in next two ingredients. Remove from heat and stir in vanilla. Place logs on oiled greaseproof paper and spoon glaze over logs immediately. Roll or sprinkle on crushed roasted nuts or seeds. (If you wait to cover logs, the glaze will harden into fudge.)

## Almond Rolls

1/2 cup roasted almonds
1/4 cup almond butter
4 Tbsp. concentrated sweetener
1 tsp. vanilla

1/4 tsp. miso
1-1/2 Tbsp. roasted carob flour
1-1/2 Tbsp. grated lemon rind
Roasted sesame seeds

Blend roasted nuts while warm. Set aside. Combine next four ingredients and beat until ball forms. Stir in next three ingredients and knead several minutes, adding blended nuts. Place mixture on greaseproof or waxed paper and roll into log. Allow to set 15 minutes before cutting into small pieces. Roll in sesame seeds before serving.

**Macadamia** (*Proteaceae*)
The Macadamia nut is a large round seed that grows on a tropical Australian evergreen tree. Macadamia trees were brought to Hawaii in the late 1800s and today it is one of Hawaii's most important crops.

The Macadamia nut has such a hard shell, that it has to be cracked by a special machine. The white kernels are usually roasted in oil, which are then very often canned and salted. Their taste is similar to a Brazil nut. They can be used in various ways and are most adaptable in cakes, candy and ice cream. The macadamia tree grows more than 40 feet tall and has dark green, leathery leaves and creamy-white flowers.

## Carob Squares

1/4 cup concentrated sweetener
1/2 cup peanut butter
1/2 cup carob powder

1/2 cup roasted finely chopped macadamia nuts
3/4 cup finely chopped currants or dates
2 tsp. coriander powder
1/2 Tbsp. miso
1/2 cup coconut

Combine sweetener and peanut butter in a saucepan, and cook over a low heat until melted. Remove from heat, and immediately stir in remaining ingredients except coconut. Press mixture into oiled and paper lined (greaseproof is best) tray. Sprinkle surface with coconut, and press into candy. Cover and chill until firm. Cut into squares to serve.

# 10. FANTASTICALLY FAST FILLERS

I know that there are those moments when you can't be bothered waiting for a dessert to bake, cool or set, because there just isn't enough time. That's the reason I have developed some "fast" food ideas, which can be used in place of a dessert when they are to be eaten in a hurry. One shouldn't gulp down any food, let alone sweets, but sometimes time gets in the way of your better judgment; so, "drink it instead."

These drink ideas are filling enough for a meal in themselves, or for a quick summer refresher on a hot day. They are also handy when you just want a quick pick-me-up!

# Forget Me Knots

1. The amount of liquid necessary for each drink will differ each time, according to the fat and oil content of each nut, seed, bean or grain, the moisture in the room, the weather of the day and how fine you are able to grind your "milk" base.
2. When nuts are warm, always blend them with warm liquid.
3. Use a small amount of liquid when blending nuts or seeds at first, so they can break down into a creamy consistency.
4. You can prepare "milk" several days in advance and keep refrigerated until you want to flavor it.
5. Experiment with different fruits when they come into season for a nice refreshing change.
6. These drinks with thick nut, seed, grain, or bean bases, can be turned into a delightful, creamy pies by just adding agar-agar. Follow one of the recipes. Shred agar-agar into 1/2 cup juice, cook until it dissolves and combine with the rest of the ingredients. Pour into pre-baked pie shell and cool until set!

# Recipes

**Oat** (*Avena sativa*)
The use of the oat is believed to date back to the European Bronze Age. Today oats are usually used to feed livestock. Humans eat them in the form of breakfast cereals. Oats possess a special quality: when cooked with four or five times the amount of liquid, they become glutenous and make a fine substitute for milk and milk puddings.

## Milk Bases: Nut, Grain and Bean

These "milks" can be used in the same way as goat's or cow's milk with much the same results. In some recipes, you may want to adjust the flavoring to compensate for the difference in taste.

### Soy Milk

Soy milk may be used for hot or cold drinks; but when added to boiling liquid, it has a tendency to curdle.

> 1 cup soybeans
> 2 qts. water
> 4 cups water

Soak beans at room temperature in 2 qts. of water until they are three times the original size (6–8 hours in warm weather or 10–12 hours in cold weather). Drain the beans, and combine them with 2 to 2-2/3 cups of water in blender and purée until very smooth. Heat 1/2 cup water in large pot; when water is very hot, add puréed beans.

Cook on medium heat, stirring constantly or beans will stick to the bottom of the pot. When foam suddenly rises to the top, turn off immediately and pour through muslin cloth, twist closed, and press sack of beans against colander or strainer to press out milk.

Pour milk into cooking pot and bring to a boil, stirring constantly to prevent sticking. Reduce heat and simmer 7–10 minutes. Serve hot or cold. If you are using organic soybeans, the milk may be slightly bitter. Add 10 percent tahini, as well as other flavorings, to cancel bitterness.

The part that is leftover is called *okara* and is very rich in nutrients. Try using it in breads, cakes, burgers, casseroles, soups, and pastes.

### Almond Milk

> 1/2 cup blanched almonds (p. 16)
> 2 Tbsp. date purée or 1 Tbsp. concentrated sweetener
> 1-1/2 cups apple juice or water (boiling)

Blanch almonds, and place in blender with date purée and 1/2 cup boiling juice or water. Blend until creamy, slowly adding the remaining liquid.

### Cashew Milk

> 1/2 cup lightly roasted cashews
> 2 Tbsp. date purée or 1 Tbsp. concentrated sweetener
> 1-1/2 cups boiling apple juice or water

Roast cashews and follow recipe for almond milk.

# Oat Milk

1/2 cup rolled oats
4–5 cups apple juice or water
Pinch of sea salt

Bring apple juice to a boil. Add oats, cover and simmer over low heat for 20 minutes. Blend all together when hot.

# Sunflower Seed Milk

1/2 cup sunflower seeds
2 Tbsp. date purée (p. 64)
2-1/2 cups boiling apple juice or water

Follow same method as cashew milk.

# Amazake Milk

See p. 161.

**Apricot** (*Prunus armeniaca*)
The apricot comes from a tree, 20 to 30 feet high, with white and sometimes pink flowers, which bloom in March or April before the leaves appear. Under proper conditions, the apricot tree can be grown from discarded pits. The trees are found mainly in warm, temperate climates. Some of the fruits are pale yellow, but they may range from yellow to deep orange with a freckled skin.

# Shakes

## Orange Shakes

2 glasses "milk"
Juice of 1 orange
1 tsp. orange rind
2 egg yolks
1 tsp. vanilla
2 Tbsp. date purée

Blend all ingredients together.

## Strawberry Shake

2 glasses "milk"
1 cup strawberries
2 Tbsp. tahini
1 tsp. cinnamon
Pinch of sea salt

Blend all ingredients together. (Strawberries may thin out shake, so use less liquid when making "milk.")

## Carob Shake

2 glasses "milk"
2 Tbsp. tahini
2 tsp. grain coffee
1 Tbsp. carob powder
1 tsp. cinnamon
1 tsp. vanilla
Pinch of sea salt

Blend all ingredients together.

*Fruit Combinations for Shakes
and Smoothies*
Apple—strawberry
Apple—carrot juice
Apple—date—sultana
Melon
Apple—peach
Apricot—date

Lemon—apple
Orange—pear
Pear—apple

**Lemon tree** (*Citrus limon*)
The lemon tree is native to south-eastern Asia, but it is grown commercially in the countries around the Mediterranean Sea and in southern California. The tree is a small evergreen with spreading branches that give it an irregular shape. It has long, pointed, pale green leaves and large fragrant flowers that usually grow in clusters. The buds tend to be reddish purple, but the flower petals are white.

## Smoothies

These drinks are somewhat thinner than shakes, but are still quite tasty and refreshing. Fresh fruit can be used in these drinks instead of apple juice, but if you are short of fruit or it is not in season, try using juice instead.

## Apple Lemon

1/2 cup cashew milk
1/2 cup apple juice
1/2 cup grated apples
1 tsp. cinnamon
1 tsp. lemon rind
1 Tbsp. lemon juice

Pinch of sea salt or *shoyu*

Blend all ingredients together.

## Apricot Peach

1/2 cup almond milk
1/2 cup apple juice
1/2 cup cooked apricots
1/2 cup fresh peaches
1 tsp. cinnamon
2 Tbsp. concentrated sweetener
Pinch of sea salt or *shoyu*

Blend all ingredients together.

## Other Drinks

### Natural Sodas

A thinner drink for those who are so inclined! Just combine sparkling mineral water and fruit concentrate or apple juice together. For extra flavor, try adding lemon, orange rind, or vanilla.

### Amazake Drink

2 cups freshly cooked sweet brown or brown rice flour
4 cups water
2 cups *koji* (yeast) rice

In freshly cooked rice, add 4 cups water and bring to a boil. Lower heat and simmer 5 minutes. Let cool to 200°F, then add 2 cups yeast rice to the first mixture.

Cover and place in a 200°F oven for 8–10 hours. Taste for sweetness. Leave longer if not sweet enough.

Pour into saucepan, add the same amount of water, bring to a boil and serve.

To use as a sweetener, after allowing rice to ferment, boil down until thick. Place in glass jar until ready to use. Amazake can be blended for a smoother texture, and used as a topping over cakes or slices.

### Rice (*Oryza sativa*)

Rice was a staple food of China as early as 2800 B.C. Most rice is produced and used in Asia; it is grown from the equator to as far north as Japan. Rice, usually grown in water, forms a hollow stem that lets oxygen pass downward and reach the roots of the wetted soil. In the milling process, the inedible outer husk is first removed.

This leaves brown rice, containing the bran, where all of the essential vitamins and minerals are stored. It is an excellent nurtritious food that can be cooked easily by simply boiling. Another variety, known as "glutinous" or sweet brown rice, is sweeter and stickier than brown rice. It is used in Japan and China mainly for festive occasions, in the form of sweet white rice.

"White" rice is brown rice with most of the valuable part of the grain—the bran—removed. Milled to remove the bran, the rice is then subjected to a process known as pearling, leaving a white grain. It is then coated with glucose and talc to

preserve the whiteness and marketed.

Rice, whether it be boiled, steamed, baked or fried, is a basic dish in many countries. Served in Asia with vegetables, in India with curry, and in Spain with fish, rice also provides the Japanese with their staple grain, *sake* (rice wine) made from fermented grains, and rice paper made from the stems.

# APPENDIX

## Sweetness Equivalency Chart

Most of the times when I prepare desserts, I choose the sweetener I use according to what kind of taste I would like: very sweet or less sweet. Sometimes I use what happens to be in the pantry at that time. Since I do a lot of experimenting, I like to vary the sweeteners and to try to get different effects in taste, texture and degree of sweetness.

When I am cooking for my family, they like their desserts less sweet, so when I have invited guests I tend to use a bit more.

This chart is designed to help you substitute one natural sweetener for another, and begin to understand the relationship among them in terms of sweetness. Remember, always *decrease* or *increase* the amount of liquid or flour in the recipe according to the liquid content of the sweetener.

In all recipes, 1/2 cup concentrated sweetener = 1/2 cup maple syrup
1/2 cup honey
1/4 cup molasses
3/4 cup sugar (not recommended)
1-1/4 cups maltose
1-1/2 cups barley malt extract
1/2 cup fruit concentrate
1 cup apple butter
1-1/4 cups date purée
1-1/2 cups grain syrup
2 cups apple juice

1) When using any concentrated sweetener in place of sugar in an ordinary recipe, reduce liquid content in recipe by 1/4 cup. If no liquid is called for in recipe, add 3–5 Tbsp. of flour for each 3/4 cup of concentrated sweetener.

2) Be sure to heat concentrated sweetener before working with it, and oil measuring cup and spoon before measuring (not necessary for apple butter, juice and date purée).

3) When barley malt extract is used, it may liquefy the consistency of the mixture, because some contain a starch splitting enzyme. This will more likely occur when eggs are not used. To compensate, bring the malt to a boil, and hold 2–3 minutes. Cool and use. This will inactivate the enzyme.

There are certain recipes that call for ingredients that you may not have, or are not familiar with. Here is a handy reference chart, to bridge the gap.

1 Tbsp. miso=1/2 tsp. salt
2 Tbsp. *shoyu*=1 Tbsp. miso
1 cup whole wheat flour minus 2 Tbsp.=1 cup white flour
1/4 tsp. dried herbs=1 tsp. fresh herbs
2 tsp. dry yeast=1 oz. compressed fresh yeast
1 bar agar-agar=4–6 Tbsp. flakes
1 bar agar-agar=1/2 Tbsp. powder
1 cup carob=1-1/2 cups cocoa
3/4 Tbsp. carob=1 square chocolate
1 cup peanut butter=315 grams
1 cup tahini=250 grams

When using tahini in recipes (especially in candy), it may be necessary to decrease the liquid content of the recipe by 1/4 cup, or add a few Tbsp. of dry ingredients (carob, spices, crushed nuts) to absorb excess oil from tahini.

## Ingredient Measurement Chart I

| | | |
|---|---|---|
| Almonds, whole, shelled | 3 cups | 1 pound |
| Almonds, ground | 2-3/4 cups | 1 pound |
| Almonds, slivered | 3 cups | 1 pound |
| Almond butter | 1-3/4 cups | 1 pound |
| Apples, cored and sliced | 3–4 cups | 1 pound |
| Apricots, dried | 3 cups | 1 pound |
| Arrowroot | 3-1/2 cups | 1 pound |
| Brown rice flour | 3-1/2 cups | 1 pound |
| Chestnut flour | 3 cups | 1 pound |
| Oats (rolled) | 4 cups | 1 pound |
| Oil | 2 cups | 1 pound |
| Peanuts, shelled | 2-1/4 cups | 1 pound |
| Peanut butter | 1-1/2 cups | 1 pound |
| Pecans, shelled | 3-1/2 cups | 1 pound |
| Raisins | 3-1/2 cups | 1 pound |
| Rye flour | 4 cups | 1 pound |
| Sea salt | 1 cup | 1 pound |
| Sesame butter | 2 cups | 1 pound |
| Strawberries (fresh) | 3 cups | 1 pint |
| Tahini | 2 cups | 1 pound |
| Walnuts, shelled, whole | 4 cups | 1 pound |
| Water | 2 cups | 1 pound |
| Whole wheat flour | 3-3/4 cups | 1 pound |
| Whole wheat pastry flour | 4 cups | 1 pound |

## Ingredient Measurement Chart II

| | | |
|---|---|---|
| Apples (raw) | 3-1/2–4 pounds | 1 pound (dried) |
| Dried fruit | 1 cup (dried) | 2 cups (soaked) |
| Eggs (whole) | 1 cup | 5 eggs |
| Agar-agar | 2 bars | 8 Tbsp. (flakes) |
| Lemon rind (dried) | 1/2–1 Tbsp. | 1 medium lemon |
| Lemon rind (fresh) | 1–2 Tbsp. | 1 medium lemon |
| Lemon juice | 3–4 Tbsp. | 1 medium lemon |
| Mint tea | 1 tsp. | 3–4 cups |
| Mu tea | 1 package | 8–10 cups |
| Orange rind (dried) | 1–2 Tbsp. | 1 medium orange |
| Orange rind (fresh) | 2–3 Tbsp. | 1 medium orange |
| Orange juice | 6–8 Tbsp. | 1 medium orange |
| Vanilla (pure-liquid) | 1 tsp. | 2-1/2-inch bean |
| Whole wheat pastry flour | 1 cup (unsifted) | 1-1/3 cup (sifted) |
| Yeast | 2 tsp (dried) | 1 ounce (compressed) |

## Temperatures for Baking Pies

| *Pie* | *Minutes* | *Oven Temperature Fahrenheit* |
|---|---|---|
| Unfilled pie shells | 15–20 | 375°–400° |
| Filled one crust cream or custard type half baked shell | 25–30 | 350° |
| Filled one crust cream or custard type | 15–20 | 350° |
| Filled two crust cream or custard type | 40–50 | 350° |
| Filled one crust fruit, half baked shell | 30–40 | 375° |
| Filled two crust fruit, unbaked shell | 45–60 | 350°–375° |
| Filled lattice top halfed, baked shell | 30–45 | 350° |
| Meringues | 45 | 225° |
| | 25 | 325° |
| | 10–12 | 400° |

Baking time will vary according to the material of the pie pan. If you use enamelware or glass, reduce the baking time indicated by one quarter; if using stoneware, increase the baking time by one half.

# Metric Equivalency Chart

1/4 lb.=113 grams
1/2 lb.=225 grams
3/4 lb.=339 grams
1 lb.=454 grams

4-1/2–5 cups=1 liter
4 cups=1 quart

| Inches | Centimeters | Millimeters |
|--------|-------------|-------------|
| 1 | 2.54 | 25.4 |
| 2 | 5.08 | 50.8 |
| 3 | 7.62 | 76.2 |
| 4 | 10.16 | 101.6 |
| 5 | 12.70 | 127.0 |
| 6 | 15.24 | 152.4 |
| 7 | 17.78 | 177.8 |
| 8 | 20.32 | 203.2 |
| 9 | 22.86 | 228.6 |
| 10 | 25.40 | 254.0 |
| 11 | 27.94 | 279.4 |
| 12 | 30.48 | 304.8 |
| 13 | 33.02 | 330.2 |
| 14 | 35.56 | 355.6 |
| 15 | 38.10 | 381.0 |

# WHERE TO SHOP

*NATURAL FOOD STORE*—Whole meal flours, grains, seeds, beans, unrefined and cold pressed oils, miso, *shoyu*, sea salt, kuzu, arrowroot, nut butters, unsulphured dried fruits, concentrated sweeteners, teas, grain coffee, fruit juices, bean curd (tofu), organic fruits and vegetables, free-range eggs, herbs, spices, etc.

*HEALTH FOOD STORE*—Basically the same selection as the natural food store, but concentration is sometimes more pronounced on "vitamin and mineral supplements."

*ORIENTAL FOOD STORE* (JAPANESE, KOREAN, CHINESE)—Dried beans, grains, spices, herbs, maltose, nuts, seeds, oils, dried chestnuts, etc.

*MIDDLE EASTERN STORE*—Herbs, spices, grains, dried beans, tahini, nuts, seeds, olive oil, goat or sheep cheese, etc.

*ITALIAN DELICATESSEN*—Dried beans, nuts, olive oil, grain, chestnut flour, unprocessed goat and sheep cheese, fresh or dried herbs, etc.

*SUPERMARKETS*—Whole grains, dried beans, whole meal flour, nuts, seeds, nut butters, herbs, spices, apple juice, cider, honey, etc.

Unfortunately, not every item that you may wish to purchase may be found under one roof, but more and more items are being made available in your local supermarkets and small shops. It will take you time to familiarize yourself with where to find what, but this basic guide was designed with the expectation that natural food items will become more accessible in a number of places. If you can't find something, please ask for it. By creating a demand, the supply will automatically come! Experiment, and try something new. If you don't know how to use it, just ask your shopkeeper who will usually be more than willing to explain how to work with it.

# SUGESTIONS FOR FURTHER READING

Aihara, Cornellia. *The Calendar Cookbook*. Los Angeles: The George Ohsawa Macrobiotic Foundation, 1979.

Ballentine, Rudolph M.D. *Diet & Nutrition*. Pennsylvania: The Himalayan International Institute, 1978.

Bumgarner, Marlene Anne. *The Book of Whole Grains*. New York: St. Martins Press, 1977.

Deutsch, Ronald M. *Realities of Nutrition*. California: Bull Publishing Co., 1976.

Dufty, William. *Sugar Blues*. New York: A Warner Communications Company, 1975.

Duquette, Susan. *Sunburst Farm Family Cookbook*. Woodbridge Press Publishing Company, 1976.

Hurd, Frank J. D.C. and Hurd, Rosalie B.S. *Ten Talents*. Minnesota: College Press.

Kushi, Michio. *The Book of Macrobiotics*. Tokyo: Japan Publications, Inc., 1977: *The Macrobiotic Way of Natural Healing*. Boston: East-West Publications, 1978.

Macia, Rafael, *The Natural Foods and Nutrition Handbook*. New York: Perennial Library, Harper & Row, 1972.

Robertson, Laurel; Flinders, Carol; Godfrey, Bronwen. *Laurel's Kitchen*. Bantam Books, Nilgiri Press, 1976.

Sussman, Vic. *The Vegetarian Alternative*. Pennsylvania: Rodale Press, 1978.

# INDEX